MAI

M

M

ISLAM IN AFRICA

ITS EFFECTS—RELIGIOUS, ETHICAL, AND SOCIAL—UPON THE PEOPLE OF THE COUNTRY

BY

ANSON P. ATTERBURY

Pastor of the Park Presbyterian Church, New York

WITH INTRODUCTION BY

F. F. ELLINWOOD

Professor of Comparative Religion, New York University

NEGRO UNIVERSITIES PRESS
NEW YORK

Originally published in 1899
by G. P. Putnam's Son, New York

Reprinted 1969 by
Negro Universities Press
A DIVISION OF GREENWOOD PUBLISHING CORP.
NEW YORK

SBN 8371-2064-0

INTRODUCTION

THE true character of the Oriental religions has never been so widely discussed as at the present time. There have been two extremes in the treatment of these systems, and it is of the very first importance that well considered and candidly presented truth respecting them should be laid before the public. The idea that Islam is wholly an imposture, destitute of all true ethics, wholly opposed through all its history to enlightenment, and breathing only cruelty and destruction, and that it is therefore unworthy of serious study, should be laid aside as not only unjust, but as productive of harm so far as it is untrue and misleading. Partly by way of reaction from this intolerant position, many apologists of the system have gone to an opposite extreme of laudation; and this has been carried to such an extent that it may now be

iii

said to be the fashion to exalt Islam and to
claim that it is a sort of preparatory school by
which such countries as Africa, for example,
may most successfully be brought to an ultimate
civilisation.

The work prepared by Rev. Anson P. Atterbury, D.D., Ph.D., on African Mohammedanism,
is therefore most timely ; and after a careful
perusal I have not hesitated to request its pub-
lication. It strikes me as eminently fair in its
treatment. It is also thorough, being characterised by a conscientious examination of facts
and the authorities by which they are given.
The works of Mr. R. Bosworth Smith, Canon
Taylor, and Dr. Edward Blyden, on the one
hand, and the writings of Livingstone, Stanley,
the late Bishop Crowther, Cardinal Lavigerie,
and many others on the other, have presented
so many contradictions in regard to the influence of Islam upon the northern and central
portions of Africa that the public mind is more
or less involved in doubt. Is it the part of wis-
dom to leave Africa for a time at least to the
aggressive influence of Mohammedanism, as
Canon Taylor has advised, and to trust to its

known hostility to intemperance as the best and most effective barrier against the trade of so - called Christian nations in intoxicating liquors? Shall we allow Mohammedan propagandism along the whole southern border of Eastern and Western Soudan to take the place of Bantu superstitions among the races lying south of them, in the belief that Islam is better than fetichism and the wholesale murder induced by witchcraft? Or shall the Christian world put forth strenuous efforts for those superstitious tribes ere Mohammedanism shall have fixed its stamp of fanaticism and bigotry upon them, rendering it thereafter far more difficult to reach them with civilising agencies?

It is such considerations as these that render the work of Dr. Atterbury timely and important. In his earlier chapters he has given such general attention to the rise and character of Islam and its author as seems necessary in opening the way to the particular questions which he has treated farther on. His estimate and judgment of Mohammed himself will not be considered severe by any candid man. If he errs in any respect it is on the side of charity. His survey

of the African field, the race divisions of its
population, the aggressive tendencies of the
Mohammedan peoples, and the more or less
helpless condition of the tribes which they are
invading, is full of instruction. The theatre
of the great conflict which seems to lie in the
immediate future is well and graphically presented.

The real vital questions, which are ably discussed in the later chapters, are such as these :
What is the character of Mohammedan propagandism in Africa? Is it a peaceful missionary
work, actuated by a sincere desire of devoted
men to raise up superstitious tribes to a knowledge of the one only true God, with correspond-
ing efforts to bring them to a high degree of
thrift and a participation in all the blessings of
civilisation? Or is it for the most part a re-
morseless and bloody conquest, either by ambi-
tious adventurers like Samadu in the West, act-
ing under the cloak of religious propagandism,
or by the still worse impulse of unscrupulous
and cruel slave raiders like Tippu Tip and others
on the Congo and throughout Eastern Africa?
It seems to me that the facts presented by Dr.

Atterbury are conclusive on this point. He is sustained, not only by the testimony of numerous travellers, as well as of missionaries, but by the current records of the newspaper press as they have come to us from time to time in the last decade.

It is confessed that the arraignment of Western nations for the great evils connected with the wholesale traffic in ardent spirits on the Congo and in the ports of West Africa is just, and difficult to answer, if regard be had to nations and governments as such. But the great difference between the wrongs inflicted by a certain element in this country and in Europe on the one hand, and the high philanthropic and benevolent interest and effort of the Christian Church of every denomination on the other, is one which it seems exceedingly difficult to impress either upon Mohammedans in the East or upon their apologists in the West. There is a vast difference between the liquor traffic on the West Coast and the slave traffic in the East, in the fact that the whole weight of Christian influence lies against the liquor traffic, while the influence of Mohammedanism is on the side of the slave trade between Africa and that sacred land of Islam, Arabia. The Koran itself encourages the capture of female slaves, at least by those who are engaged in war for the standard of Islam ; and the present status of slavery in Arabia and other Mohammedan countries is in a line with the whole history of Islam and the example of the prophet. It justifies itself by the teaching of his alleged inspirations, and the policy pursued through the long history of the system in many lands and through many centuries. Slavery is the great industry of Mohammedans in Eastern Africa, and even the Muftis and sacred teachers of Islam are engaged in the traffic. Slavery is a part of Islam ; the liquor trade is no part of Christianity. There are apologists among us who, emboldened by a sort of popular encouragement which has not been wanting of late, venture to claim that Mohammedanism has done and is doing more for civilisation than Christianity. It is useless to enter into elaborate argument on this point. The desolations of Northern Africa, once populous, now scarcely accessible to travellers without military escort, the long caravan routes

strewn with bleaching bones of slaves, the desolation and depopulation of whole districts east
of the African lakes as well as on the borders of
the Great Desert—these must respond to the
allegation that Islam moves in the forefront of
civilisation, and sows broadcast the seeds of
prosperity and peace among men.

F. F. ELLINWOOD.

PREFACE

PERHAPS the writer was the better prepared to undertake this investigation from some personal observation of Mohammedanism in India, Egypt, and the Turkish Empire. But the work here attempted is such as no man could qualify himself to perform merely by ordinary travelling ; it would be hard, or impossible, for one to reach so widely in personal experience as to be prepared thereby to speak concerning the varied Mohammedanism of the African continent. Limited personal experience would, necessarily, make one's presentation of the subject partial and prejudiced. To take the statements of many men, to weigh testimony and reconcile or reject contradiction, to estimate and allow for personal prejudice—to view the field as a whole—is work to be done only at a distance, and calmly in one's study.

It is surprising to find how largely an investigation of this subject, and similar subjects, must depend upon the lives and labours of Christian missionaries for reliable information. It is only another proof of the valuable collateral benefits rendered by foreign missionary effort.

The manuscript of this work was sent to Rev. F. F. Ellinwood, D.D., Secretary of the Presbyterian Board of Foreign Missions and Professor of Comparative Religions in New York University. In a private letter Dr. Ellinwood makes some remarks concerning Mohammedanism which it is important to present, as possibly balancing what may seem to some an unduly favourable estimate of the prophet and his religion in the first chapter of this book. He writes :

" In one or two points I am compelled to differ from your favourable estimate of Mohammed as contained in the first chapter. Since I returned the MS. I have read over the Koran anew. I am more and more impressed with its pettifogging character. Every sura seems to have been written for some personal object, and not from any divine constraint. What a contrast to the old prophets,

Preface

who were *driven* to the disinterested utterance of
unwelcome messages ! There is no 'Woe is me !'
but there is a lust to be justified, or a defeat (as at
Ohad) to be palliated, or a victory (as at Bedr) to
be made capital of, or there is a dig to be given to
the people of Mecca, or a curse to be administered
to the Koreish; or a weak point in the faith is to be
patched, or a robbery of caravans is to be justified,
or the blind bravery of his soldiers is to be stimulated by some new promise of heavenly houris who
'shall always remain virgins.' I find that the
threats of hell are repeated some hundreds of
times, and generally against those who do not pin
their faith to ' *me* '. And they are placed in such
settings and expressed in such a questionable spirit
as to seem not the solemn utterances of a real
prophet, but the mere hard swearing of an unscrupulous adventurer, who has an object to gain.
The Old Testament scriptures are used, not as
utterances of the voice of God and for their own
sake, but always as means to an end. Where are
there any psalms of devotion or prayers of spiritual aspiration ? As to the New Testament, the
Apocryphal Gospels are preferred,—a fact which
shows more of sharp practice than of sincerity.
I cannot regard Mohammed as a real prophet.
Though he was a man of power, he was corrupted
by his own revelations."

A. P. A.

New York,
January, 1899.

CONTENTS

Contents

CHAPTER V

The Mohammedan Conquest of Africa . 55

Contents

CHAPTER VI

Contents

Contents

CHAPTER VIII

Contents

In general the change from paganism so small as to amount to nothing—Even the Bedeyat are merely nominal Moslems—The negro tribes that have been won to allegiance are Moslem in little more than name—The Bournous, Fulahs, Mandingoes, and their

CHAPTER X

Contents   xxiii

Contents

ISLAM IN AFRICA

ISLAM IN AFRICA

CHAPTER I

MOHAMMED

ABOUT the beginning of the seventh century Mohammed appeared, claiming for
himself the dignity of a prophet of the only
and true God. He was a true prophet; rather,
he was a prophet of some truth. God sent him
forth with a message. He delivered it; but he
added to it human elements. He was a prophet;
but not in that full meaning of the term under
which the prophets of the Old Testament cried,
" Thus saith the Lord ! " We may not believe
that he was a prophet in that sense in which
Mohammed claimed for himself the honour—
" There is one God and Mohammed is His

prophet." But he grasped the great truth of
God as the one eternal ruler of angels and men,
and he uttered that truth from God to man.
He who in an age and country of idolatry saw
God as the One Supreme, and told his fellow
men thereof, was truly called of God.

The idea of the ONE GOD—the vision of
Him, whether merely by mental grasp or in
true ecstasy—is the greatest and most essential
that the mind of man can receive. With it,
man can mount upon the summits of heaven,
can hold communion with the All in All. Without it, man wanders in mist and mire, searching
vainly for the satisfaction of his soul's innate
need. This was the sublime thought, or vision,
that possessed the whole being of Mohammed.
Partly from tradition, but largely from hints
given in the Koran itself, we may gather the
story of his vision and call. He was about
forty years of age. For some time mental
gloom, a. olute melancholy, had been pressing
upon him terribly. We are not told as to the
lines in which his morbid thoughts ran; but
from the marked result of that crisis in his
life we may readily infer that with which his

thoughts, his soul, wrestled. As with many
another less strong, less fortunate, groper after
truth, the man was pondering deeply those vast
problems which centre around the idea and being of God. He was grappling with suggestions of truth and duty that he could hardly
understand and from which deeply he shrank.
It seems to have been his custom, as with some
of his countrymen, to spend a certain month in
retirement and meditation. At an hour's walk
from Mecca, there is a mountain, " a huge bar-
ren rock," wherein is a cave in which Mohammed spent the days of that fateful time of
seclusion about the year 610 A.D. In the bald,
ghostly solitude of that desolate rock, with
fasting and prayer, under the pressure of his
deep melancholy, in circumstances most favourable to a recurrence of his physical malady,
there came the vision and the call. It was in
the middle of the night that the angel Gabriel
appeared to him, so he claimed[1]: " Verily we
sent down the Koran in the night of al Kadr.
And what shall make thee understand how ex-

---

[1] Sale's Koran, chapter xcvii. We assume that the revelation of the Koran and the call to service are identical.

cellent the night of al Kadr is? The night of
al Kadr is better than a thousand months.
Therein do the angels descend and the spirit
Gabriel also, by the permission of their Lord,
with His decrees concerning every matter. It
is peace until the rising of the morn."

Mohammed claimed that Gabriel held before him a silken scroll,[1] and said, "Read." He
could not—probably he had never learned to
read. But in some way the words from that
scroll were graven on his heart. The voice said,
"Cry."[2] Twice the call came; and twice Mohammed struggled against the call. He was
pressed sorely, "as if a fearful weight had been
laid upon him." For the third time the voice
called, "Cry." And he said, "What shall I
cry?" There came the answer, "Cry—in the
name of thy Lord."

The prophet had received his call—trem-
blingly he went forth to fulfil it. In deep dis-
tress he came to his wife Khadija and told her
of what had occurred. True woman as she

---

[1] Koran, ch. xcvi.
[2] Essay on Islam by Emanuel Deutsch, in *Mohammed and Mohammedanism*, R. Bosworth Smith, page 306.

was, she yielded to him as prophet of God. Even yet he could not force himself to his mission. He was on the point of seeking death. It is supposed that this state of anguish lasted from two to three years. Again came one of his strange attacks, in which, as he claimed, the voice of God said,[1] "O thou covered, arise and preach, and magnify thy Lord." Henceforth there was no interruption and no doubt; he knew and obeyed his call.

Dr. Sprenger claims[2] that the answer to the medical question as to Mohammed's physical condition would give the key to the whole problem of Islam. We can hardly agree with so material a conception of a great truth and a great prophet. But it is to be clearly recognised that this physical element occupies a large place in any proper explanation of the phenomenon. Mohammed was of an excessively nervous temperament.

"The excitement under which he composed the more poetical suras of the Koran was so great—his lips were quivering and his hands shaking whilst

[1] Koran, chapter lxxiv.
[2] *Encyclopedia Britannica*, xvi., 547, Note 2.

he received the inspirations. When he was taken
ill he sobbed like a woman in hysterics. During
the battle of Bedr his nervous excitement seemed
to have bordered on frenzy. He suffered from
hallucinations; his fits were preceded by great
depression of spirits; his face was clouded; they
were ushered in by coldness of the extremities and
shivering. He shook as if he suffered from ague
and called out for covering; his mind was in a
most excited state. If the attack proceeded beyond this stage his eyes became fixed and staring,
and the motions of his head convulsive and auto-
matic. At length perspiration broke out, which
covered his face in large drops; and with this
ended the attack." [1]

Whether these attacks were epilepsy, or cata-
lepsy, or some severe form of hysteria, we cannot now know; the answer lies hidden in the
mysteries of the nervous system of man. Psy-
chic investigation of later years opens wonders
which we cannot define or understand. All
that we can say is that there was some close
connection between this ecstasy, or epilepsy, or
whatever it may have been, and the claimed
inspiration of the great prophet. He saw visions; he heard voices; these experiences were

[1] Dr. William Smith's edition of Gibbon's *Rome*. Notes
quoted from Dr. Sprenger, chapters l.–lii.

the assurance for him, and for his followers, which with mighty enthusiasm carried them over the world.

The circumstances into which he was born were such as to favour greatly his mission. There seems to have been a reaction in Arabia, about that time, from idolatry. The Hanifs, a sect of Arabs to which Mohammed belonged, were vaguely rejecting polytheism. Also, Judaism was pressing upon that region; and a corrupt form of Christianity presented itself to Mohammed in his youth. The political condition of Arabia favoured his mission; the unconquered, but divided, families and tribes of Arabia presented possibilities of combination and subjection by one of their own race. Especially fortunate was it for Mohammed that Medina seems to have been peculiarly prepared for him. When the prophet was forced to leave Mecca, he found in Medina not simply a place of refuge, but a readiness to support him. He soon raised an army with which to make counter-attack upon Mecca. He was forced into warfare. A mighty enthusiasm enabled him to triumph at the first and critical battle. Henceforth his pathway was clearly marked out and, usually, triumphant.

One thing more we must notice: the "contrast between his reverent and meditative youth, and his fierce and libidinous old-age." There are those who claim that Mohammed was an impostor from the start; but we have made it plain that we are not of that number. There are those who assert that the man, sincere at the start, became determinedly false and vicious when he took the sword into his hands and entered upon his career of conquest—a sudden and complete moral change. We would make it clear that we are not of this class of his critics—though most of his later biographers incline to the opinion that he was, more or less, a conscious impostor at the end. Again, there are those who believe that he was a hero throughout, morally. They assert that he was sincere in his belief in himself and throughout his command over his followers. They belittle the evidences of evil in his character and life. R. Bosworth Smith, Thomas Carlyle, E. A. Freeman, more or less closely approach this, in their statements of the moral problem presented in the life of Mohammed. We would separate ourselves from this class of critics, for reasons now to be given.

It is hard to see how one can now read the story of Mohammed's entrance upon his mission, can see him trembling and hesitating on the brink of what was for him an awful chasm, can go with him historically through the early years of his prophetic work, without being forced to the conclusion that this wild and forceful spokesman for God believed in himself and his message and mission with that deep sincerity which alone can carry a man through such experiences as he was forced to enter. Whatever may be one's opinion as to the divine authority of Mohammed and his mission at the start, no one can successfully deny that the man then thought himself the prophet of God and that the teachings that he presented were the truth of God. Mohammed started on his mission with a deep and intense sincerity: "Though the sun at my right hand and the moon at my left were to command me to give up this matter, I would not give it up."[1]

[1] Quoted by Dr. Henry P. Smith in *The Bible and Islam*,

Now we would claim that this sincerity continued throughout. And yet startling decline, moral contradiction in an ordinary man absolutely incomprehensible, characterised the later years of his life. In him is presented the awful profanity of a man who would call upon God to justify his sensuality, who would bring down God in writing to establish unrighteousness. Surely never has high mission been so prostituted. Of the one hundred and fourteen suras in the Koran, more were written to justify Mohammed's personal ambition, unrighteousness, lust, and sensuality than some of his biographers would care to allow. Using his authority as spokesman for God, he dared impiously to justify and establish deeds of the devil.

Yet throughout the worst of his moral degradation he seems to have appealed freely to the Supreme Being, and to have rested confidently upon his own integrity. "We are only two," said his trembling companion to Mohammed, at a time when his pursuers were seeking eagerly

p. 15, Scribners, 1897. See his estimate of Mohammed's character: " In this persistence in his calling Mohammed is not unworthy of being compared with the Old-Testament prophets," p 15.

for him as he was hid in the cave. "There is a third," said Mohammed ; " it is God Himself." That, though before the period of his moral inconsistency, was the characteristic of his life throughout. " I seek refuge in the light of Thy countenance alone "—that seemed ever his thought. Even in the overwhelming pressure of the death hour, when men most clearly reveal their true selves, whatever they may have seemed to others in previous years, he evidenced the same majestic assurance with which he began. He believes that God has spoken to him ; he is assured that what he has spoken for God is divinely authorised ; he believes that "there is one God and Mohammed is His prophet."

We would not belittle the moral weakness of the man. Dr. Ellinwood, in this connection, well presents the truth that "the test of character lies in its trend." The trend of that man's character was, during the last ten years of his life, definitely, toward the bad. Nothing can be more clear than that the man descended into sin so gross and unrighteousness so terrible that, if these isolated acts certainly

in dicatea permanent condition of will, he became bad indeed. Yet we cannot reconcile
with this the evidences of his continued self-
assurance in any way other than by supposing
that this strange man, unaccountably catching
gleams of divine glory in moments of epileptic
frenzy, is not to be judged fully as other men.
There seem to have been possibilities of moral
contradiction in him that we cannot allow for
an ordinary man. We must simply accept the
moral contradiction: he was good, yet bad;
he was sincere, yet sensual. He must have
thought, in the wild fancies of his imagined
communion with the divine, that God authorised the foul adultery of his marriage with the
Egyptian Mary. In his mental and physical
constitution were possibilities of moral inconsistency such as do not, in ordinary men, exist
to like degree. Most men can persuade themselves, at times, that doubtful wrong is really
right; he was a man the extravagances of
whose nature were such that, under the temp-
tation of lust and in the moral enervation of
power and success, he could really believe that
God rebuked him for undue continence.

In Mohammed we have the picture of a man grasping a great truth, giving himself up to it completely, heroically. We behold a character in which enthusiasm controls; working in a bodily frame in which some form of nervous excitation produced trance-like experiences in which visions and voices were perceived. Taking the great truth as evidence that these epileptic intimations were divine, struggling for a something that he knew to be right, forced by circumstances into a life of warfare and political management, in increasing age and power yielding evermore to the lower passions and ambitions within him, in a strangely disordered soul identifying his own desires and ambitions with the divine will, throughout he produced what he forced others to think were real revelations from God, even to the justification of his own evil. He lay in that border land of psychical and spiritual experience wherein a strong, yet disordered, intellect seeks to obey God and yet gratify self—at bottom sincere throughout, yet terribly under the control of the evil within himself. In it all we have a startling illustration of the possibilities of the

co-existence of the devilish and the divine in a
man.   He was so strangely great that a moral
contradiction, impossible to the same degree in
an ordinary man, lay hid within his soul.

CHAPTER II

ISLAM

THE word "Islam" has two meanings: one refers to the religious system of Mohammed, the other to the Mohammedan world. Islam means the doctrine, or the disciples, of Mohammed. Let us look at each of these meanings.

The Koran is the Bible of the Mohammedans; an infallible rule of faith and practice from which there can be no appeal.[1] It is not the only rule of life[2]: Mohammedan tradition is of great authority,[3] and the successors to the leadership of the great prophet have done something towards determining doctrine and

[1] *Encyclopedia of Missions*, ii., 117.
[2] *The Missionary Review of the World*, v., 137.
[3] In general, on the Koran and Mohammedan tradition. See *Faith of Islam*, by E. Sell, ch. i. and ii.

duty. But in general the Koran is the particular and permanent message from God to man, through the greatest and most favoured of His servants, Mohammed. Each word, each letter, was directly inspired : an extreme theory of verbal inspiration obtains acceptance throughout the Mohammedan world.

The book is a wonderful one, not so much in its contents as in its origin, its history and its influence. The faithful believe that the original text existed in heaven. An angel brought it down piece by piece to the prophet; he in turn proclaimed it to the world. It is not large—somewhat smaller than the Christian's Bible; but it will seem long to most non-Mohammedans who attempt to read it through. Chapter by chapter it was revealed, so they claim, often in direct connection with one of the startling fits of nervous frenzy to which the prophet was subject. Towards the end of his life these revelations seemed to come suspiciously in connection with the prophet's political needs or personal desires ; he would find himself so placed that the authority of God was needed to sustain his position, so

most opportunely a revelation would be made
to fit the occasion. While some of the suras
are evidently wrought in the fierce fire of
frenzy, it is quite as evident that the greater
part of the book "is undoubtedly the result
of deliberation"; many passages are based on
purely intellectual reflection.[1] But however it
may have originated, Mohammedans the world
over praise it as a book beyond compare.
Mohammed himself claimed that the only
miracle in connection with his assertions, the
only miraculous proof needed for his mission,
was the Koran. Some Arabic scholars, not
Mohammedans, have said that in the original
language it is indeed poetical and impressive;
to most of those who read it in a translation
it will seem exceedingly uninteresting and
uninspiring.

We are told that Mohammed dictated these
"revelations" to a scribe; for it is at least
doubtful as to whether or not the great prophet
was able to read and write. At the time of his
death the chapters of the Koran "existed only
in scattered fragments, on bits of stone, leather,

[1] *Encyclopedia Britannica*, xvi., 598.

and bones " [1] ; but we may assume that the
memories of his adoring disciples were, chiefly,
the immaterial parchment on which were ascribed his assertions as to the words of God. It
is said that soon after the prophet's death there
were some who could recite the whole Koran,
as they then understood it, without an error.[1]
But the final establishment of the canon was
made during the caliphate of Omar, and is supposed, with great probability, to contain the
very words that were delivered by the prophet.

This is the book that has, largely, made Mohammedanism. Two hundred millions of people, more or less, reverence it even now as the
very word of God. They pore over its pages,
over each letter therein, with a worshipful attention that may be indeed sometimes a reverent heart's holy and acceptable offering unto
the Supreme Being above.

There is a translation of a letter written by
the Sheik-ul-Islam to a German convert, which
contains a statement of Mohammedan doctrine
from the highest authority in the world, and
may be taken by us as an authentic summary

[1] *Encyclopedia of Missions*, ii., 117.

of the faith of modern Islam. The following
is a condensation of its statements [1] :

" Conversion to Islamism demands no religious
formality, and hope depends upon the authorisa-
tion of no one. It is sufficient to believe and pro-
claim one's belief." " Islamism has for its basis,
faith in the unity of God, and in the mission of His
dearest servant Mohammed"—"to avow it in words,
'there is only one God, and Mohammed is His
prophet.'" " He who makes this profession of
faith becomes a Mussulman, without having need
of the consent or approbation of anyone." " Believers are all brothers."

" Man was created out of nothing to adore his
Creator." " God—in according to certain human
beings the gift of prophecy, and in so revealing the
true religion, has overwhelmed His servants with
blessings." " The book of God which descended
last from heaven is the sacred Koran, the unchange-
able teachings of which will last even to the day
of the last judgment." " The first of the prophets
was Adam ; and the last, Mohammed." "Between
these two, many others have lived ; their number
is known only to God. The greatest of all is Mohammed. After him come Jesus, Moses (and
others)."

" The day of the last judgment. The dead will
rise again—to render their accounts ; the elect

[1] The New York *Independent*, xl., 2045, p. 1. See also
Sell's *Faith of Islam*.

will be sent to Paradise ; those condemned, to Hell."

" Also it is necessary, as an article of faith, to attribute all good and all evil to the providence of God."

" But to be a perfect believer, it is necessary to perform certain duties ; to pray God—and to avoid falling into such sins as murder, robbery, etc. Besides the profession of faith—a good Mussulman ought to pray five times a day, distribute to the poor a fortieth part of his goods every year, fast during the month of Ramazan, and make once in his life a pilgrimage to Mecca."

" Faith annuls all sin. He who is converted to Islamism becomes as innocent as when first born, and he is responsible only for the sins committed after his conversion."

" A sinner who repents and asks God's forgiveness, obtains pardon. Only the rights of his neighbour are an exception to this rule ; for the servant of God who cannot obtain justice in this world reclaims his right at the day of judgment, and God, who is just, will then compel the oppressor to make restitution to the oppressed. To avoid this responsibility, the only means is to get acquittance from your neighbour whom you have wronged."

" In the Mussulman's religion there is no clergy. In all religious acts there is no mediator between God and His servants. Only the accomplishment of certain religious ceremonies, such as the prayers on Friday at Beiram, is subordinated to the will of the Caliph, of the prophet, and the Sultan of Mussulmans. Since the arrangement of ceremonies for Islamism is one of his sacred attributes, obedience to his orders is one of the most important religious duties."

"One of the things to which every Mussulman ought to be very attentive is righteousness in character. Vices such as pride, presumption, egotism, and obstinacy do not become a Mussulman. To revere the great, and to compassionate the insignificant, are precepts of Islamism."

We have thus given, with considerable fulness, the essential points in a remarkable summary of a world-wide faith. Fullest reading of Mohammedan literature will, we are persuaded from personal experience, give nothing more favourable; though there will probably be some change of proportion and emphasis of doctrine as the result. The letter of the Sheik-ul-Islam was written to a convert from Christianity, and was "evidently intended to make as favorable an impression on Christians as possible."

We should notice that in Mohammedan thought the idea of the one God stands out as overwhelming. Read the second sura of the Koran:

" God ! there is no God but He ; the living, the self-subsisting ; neither slumber nor sleep seizeth Him. To Him belongeth whatsoever is in heaven and on earth. Who is he that can intercede with Him, but through His good pleasure ? He knoweth that which is past, and that which is to come unto them, and they shall not comprehend anything of His knowledge, but so far as He pleaseth. His throne is extended over heaven and earth, and the preservation of both is no burden unto Him. He is the high and the mighty."

Throughout that celebrated sura, undignified by the title " The Cow," there is a presentation of the majesty and authority of God which is indeed impressive.

To obtain a correct idea of the emphasis and relative importance of certain doctrines and duties in Islam, we should also notice the stress laid upon prayer. " Prayer is better than sleep " were the words that Mohammed's slave Billal was accustomed to use to call the faithful to prayer at the stated times. The phrase is repeated every day throughout the Mohammedan world.[1] The call to prayer five times a day, wherever the good Mohammedan may

[1] Blyden, *Christianity, Islam, and the Negro Race*, 372.

chance to be, and in spite of all conspicuousness, is like a seal upon soul and body—fastening the believer to Islam and evidencing the divine ownership before man.

It has been well observed that "the radical fact about a religion is the way in which it grapples with the human will." [1] Absolute submission of the will to God is the fundamental idea of Mohammedanism. Indeed, the word "Islam" originally meant submission.

Notice another feature greatly emphasised; easy requirement of doctrine, united with strict assertion of practical religious duties. It is easy to say " There is only one God and Mohammed is His prophet " ; all that the believer now has to do is to keep the five observances—creed recital, prayer, fasting, almsgiving, pilgrimage. With little stress laid upon the intellectual and spiritual elements, and large emphasis and proportion given to the practical, the system is admirably adapted to prevail among men.

Further, the summary of doctrine which we have presented gives but little idea of the empha-

[1] *Shall Islam Rule Africa?* Rev. L. C. Barnes, 23.

sis with which the hope of Paradise is pressed
upon believers as an anticipation and a motive.
" All the acts of soldiers in holy war, even their
sleep, are considered as prayer." " The gate
to Paradise lies between drawn swords." In
this, largely, lies the secret of the marvellous
military success of the Mohammedan conquerors. But Paradise is represented in descriptions so material, even coarse, that it is
hard to see how disembodied spirits can find
much satisfaction therein.

It will be seen that in the summary presented
above there is little or no suggestion of that
fatalism which is usually supposed to be the
" central tenet of Islam." It seems to be true
that the practical result of Islamic doctrine is
a fatalistic tendency throughout Mohammedanism. All that happens is ordered by God.
On the other hand, the very fact that the act
of prayer is so largely emphasised would seem
to modify or contradict such fatalism. We
may assert "the absolute fallacy of the notion
that fatalism is a doctrine of the Koran ; it
teaches a very contrary doctrine." [1]   " Moham-

[1] Blyden, *Christianity, Islam, and the Negro Race*, 289.

med . . . was not what we should call a fatalist." [1] " Mohammed's whole system is one of faith, built on hope and fear." [2] Theoretically, Islam may not be fatalistic ; but practically, in large measure, it is.

" As the system became more complex and dogmatic, men lost the sense of the nearness of God. He became an unapproachable being. A harsh, unfeeling Fate took the place of the Omnipotent Ruler. It is this dark fatalism which, whatever the qurán may teach on the subject, is the ruling principle in all Muslim communities." [3]

It is a misconception on the part of many that Islam is in complete opposition to Christianity. On the contrary, as can readily be seen from what has been here presented, there are many hopeful points of contact. Indeed, so far as doctrine is concerned, the one central point of opposition is in a definition of the unity of God which excludes the Christian doctrine of the Trinity. Closely connected with this

[1] *The Bible and Islam*, Dr. Henry P. Smith (Scribners, 1897), 140, 155.

[2] Deutsch, quoted by Blyden, *Christianity, Islam, and the Negro Race*, 289.

[3] Sell, *Faith of Islam*, 240.

"heresy" are the doctrines of the authority of Mohammed and the inspiration of the Koran. But, had it not been that Mohammed evidently got a wrong idea of the Christian doctrine concerning Christ, derived from the gross doctrinal statements of a corrupt form of Christianity, it is hard to say what there might not have been of identification between the reform which he headed and the religion which Jesus Christ had established before him. Dr. Döllinger says, "Islam must be considered at bottom a Christian heresy." [1]

But in thus presenting certain essential facts and features of the doctrines of Mohammedanism, we would not be understood as taking that "rose-coloured" view of Islam that some recent writers have presented. "Canon Taylor, in a little volume entitled *Leaves from an Egyptian Note Book*, has drawn a picture of Islam which Omar and Othman would hardly have recognised." [2] Mr. R. Bosworth Smith has written a volume with the evident intent of

---

[1] *Encyclopedia of Missions*, ii., 113.
[2] *Oriental Religions and Christianity*, F. F. Ellinwood, D.D., 212.

showing that Mohammedanism is not so black as it has been painted—indeed, that it is almost white. Fairness to Mr. Smith, however, requires us to state that, when he found what misuse was made by Canon Taylor of the favourable presentation of Islam in *Mohammed and Mohammedanism*, he saw and acted upon the need of giving due emphasis to the other side of the question, thus to some degree counteracting the effect of the partial presentation made in his book.[1] Dr. Blyden is, at times, strongly inclined to eulogy in describing Islam. But however one may think concerning the authoritative doctrinal statements made by the Sheik-ul-Islam, it is certainly true that there are essential evils, sanctioned by the Koran, in Mohammedan law: polygamy, easy divorce, concubinage, slavery, the death penalty to the renegade from the faith.[2] Whoever would glorify Islam must apologise for certain social evils inherent in the system—like slow poison, paralysing the whole body.

[1] *Oriental Religions and Christianity*, F. F. Ellinwood, D.D., 217.
[2] *The Missionary Review of the World*, i., 784, 785.

Thus much we have been obliged to say concerning Islam as a system of doctrine—in order to understand what it is that has made, and now characterises, Islam as the body of disciples, particularly as existing in that part of the world on which our attention must be concentrated. For this form of religion, originating at Mecca, has extended westwardly across Africa to the Atlantic, and easterly to Northwestern China, embracing men of all the known races; and embracing them not as individuals but as " communities,—whole nations and tribes,—weaving itself into their national life and giving colour to their political and social as well as ecclesiastical existence." [1]   It is estimated that there are over two hundred million adherents.[2]   Throughout the twelve hundred years since the Hejira, in spite of temporary and local relapses, Mohammedanism has been making, on the whole, constant and startling advance.   The first century and a quarter after the death of Mohammed was a period of unexampled conquest.   Naturally there came divisions, sects, retrogression

[1] Blyden, *Christianity, Islam, and the Negro Race*, 283.
[2] *Encyclopedia of Missions*, ii., 121.

at points. But again and again has Mohammedan enthusiasm broken forth, for a while irresistibly. The great truth contained in its
doctrine of God has had vital power sufficient
to sustain the whole system, in spite of its evils,
throughout the centuries; and this has sent it
triumphantly, even in our own century, over
broad reaches of territory and in new conquest.
So startling has been this career of progress
that some have asserted that Islam is a messen-
ger of God, sent to prepare the way before His
face. We do not dare to say that; but we do
not dare wholly to deny it.

CHAPTER III

THE CONTINENT AND ITS EXPLORATION

VICTOR HUGO says, "In the twentieth century Africa will be the cynosure of all eyes ";—it is well worth our attention before that time.

The continent is nearly four times the size of the United States; its length is over four thousand miles, its extreme width four thousand miles, its area 11,864,600 square miles.[1] Its general configuration has been compared to an "inverted dish"; a rim of lowland around the edge, an elevated plateau in the centre. A slight depression in this tableland makes possible the four great lakes of the central region. Also, four great rivers force their way from the centre to the rim—the Nile, the Niger, the Congo, and the Zambesi. The nar-

[1] *The Independent*, l., 568.

row edge of coast-line is, except possibly along
the northern shore, a malarial belt, terribly
fatal to human beings whose constitutions cannot stand the attack.   But in general the interior regions are healthful.   Africa has been
called "the White Man's Grave"; but this is
not so much the fault of Africa as the white
man's ignorance.   Enlarging experience seems
to prove that with proper care the European
may live almost anywhere in Africa as health-
fully as in any region of similar latitude.   "The
climate of the Congo has been unduly vilified."
"Traders on the coast have generally fair
health."   "There is no reason why Congo
should be considered more unhealthy than
India generally."   A missionary, writing from
the region of Victoria,[1]

"found the natives themselves to be quite as subject to fevers and other ills as white men in the
same locality.   Most severe illnesses in the case of
white men in Africa arise from their own imprud-
ence or want of knowledge.   Where white men exercise care and prudence, they have been able to
live in fair health for a long period of years, even
where there has been a high mortality among the

[1] *Church at Home and Abroad*, vii., 536.

blacks in the same region. Our knowledge of the conditions injurious to health in tropical Africa is constantly increasing—chill, and malaria, is the main cause of African fever. . . . The Anglo-Saxon will outlive his black companions even in the heart of Africa." [1]

Evidently life for the white man in Africa is not so unhealthy as has been supposed.

Africa is a continent of desert and forest. Vast regions in the northern part, some large districts farther south and in the eastern part of the continent, are desolate. But irrigation is all that is needed to make the desert blossom as a rose. The numerous oases in the desert of Sahara seem to prove this. The proposition to open a canal, through which the waters of the Atlantic or the Mediterranean shall be brought into the Saharan Desert, opens fancies fascinating as a fairy tale, and as unreal.

In startling contrast with the desert regions of Africa are the vast expanses of forest, seemingly tractless and impenetrable, which cover a large part of Central Africa. The flora is exceedingly, we may say in places excessively, rich and varied—so much so as to render the

[1] Confirmed strikingly by A. R. Wallace and W. F. Blackman in *The Independent*, LI., 667.

larger part of the continent, until of late years, a sealed letter from God in nature.

The land of Ethiopia is frequently referred to in the Bible—though the designation may be used somewhat vaguely. Evidently the region south and perhaps southwest of Egypt is meant. It has been claimed that the old Egyptians were closely related to the Nigritians ; and indeed much of the sculpturing and picturing of old Egyptian civilisation would seem to indicate this. If this be true, it brings large numbers of Central Africans, now despised and down-trodden, into a grandeur of historical prominence. Vague ideas seem to have been current among the Greeks and Romans concerning Central Africa—rumours of great lakes, of the Mountains of the Moon, of dwarfs. These hints have been proved in our later days strangely accurate ; but mixed with them were wild fancies of the imagination, poets' dreams. It is evident that early Greek and Roman writers knew more of the centre of Africa than did European scholars of comparatively few years ago.

Modern exploration may be said to have be-

gun with Mr. James Bruce, who in 1768 departed
from Cairo on a journey to Abyssinia, in order
to discover the source of the Nile. After him
venturesome men in a glorious succession have
kept up the quest down to our own times. But
the real opening of the centre of the continent
has been only within the last twenty-five or
thirty years.

"All this aims to build up a great civilisation
which, if it is successful, while it will make the
white man the leader of the black man for the next
one hundred years, will do that other and grand
thing spoken of by Victor Hugo when he said
'that in the nineteenth century the white man has
made a man out of the black, and in the twentieth century Europe will make a world out of
Africa.'"

The cost of such exploration, in life rather
than in treasure, has been incalculable. Take
for illustration "that awful itinerary" of Stanley's journey to the Albert Nyanza—

"through a forest larger than France, and
through the matted undergrowths of which the
starved and dwindling column crept at the rate of
three miles a day. That awful itinerary, filled
with fever, fightings, and hideous sufferings, con-

tinued for more than five months before the one hundred and more thin skeletons emerged into the plain regions, and with food and plenty about them began to take heart and hope." [1]

But the large advance that has been made is well indicated by the simple statement that in his journey of 1876, Mr. Stanley took 991 days in first crossing Africa; but in 1888 he could go from Glasgow to Stanley Falls, nearly half across Africa and all the distance from Glasgow in addition, in forty-three days. [2] Railroad facilities are being already started; a telegraph line through the heart of Africa is planned and begun, and we have, now and then, in the columns of our daily papers, hints of commercial advantage in Africa, and suggestions of white colonisation therein, which evidence clearly the fact that the centre of Africa is becoming of absorbing interest to the overcrowded masses in the centres of Europe and of America. English, German, and French statesmen and engineers are busily engaged in trying boundary lines and defining spheres of influence.

[1] *The Missionary Review of the World*, iii., 125.
[2] *Ibid.*, i., 469.

Maps are being made that show clearly even the *minutiæ* of geographical features.

The material improvements which have been made in the last two decades have been exceedingly rapid. Facts to which particular attention is called are:

The completion of the great and difficult railroad enterprise connecting the upper Congo with the sea. Railroad traffic is now in full operation there, while above Stanley Pool there are no less than forty-five steamers, mostly small, though one of two hundred and fifty tons is now in process of transportation.

A French railroad is in progress from the Senegal, designed to connect its navigable waters with those of the upper Niger, also with Timbuctu and Western Soudan.

A railroad under Portuguese auspices from Loango to what is known as the Hinterland in Angola.

An East-Coast line under English auspices from Mombasa to the lakes is in progress; one hundred and fifty miles have already been covered; five hundred more are on the way to completion.

A South African railroad from the Cape to Kimberley and on to Buluwayo, now completed with many branches, and destined to connect with Lake Nyassa and thence by the east line of the Congo Free State with the railroad system of the Nile, which will soon reach Khartoum.

Railroads extending southward in Algiers and Tunis.

A road in German East Africa extending toward Tanganyika from Dhar-es-Salam. Telegraph lines not only accompany these railroads, but in many cases precede them.[1]

Evidently, as this year (1899) opens, Africa has already become unsealed.

[1] See *Assembly Herald*, January, 1899.

CHAPTER IV

THE NATIVE RACES

THE ethnography of Africa is difficult. There are many different races to be taken into consideration. The differences between man and man in Africa are almost, or quite, as great as between man in America and man in China. One reason for the great confusion in the European mind concerning men and matters in Africa lies in the fact that these racial distinctions are not recognised. Dr. Blyden in commenting upon an article in the *Westminster Review*[1] severely criticises the writer on this ground:

" The Westminster Reviewer chooses to select the very lowest tribes upon which to make his unfavourable comments, and from which to infer the character of the whole race. . . . Such is the

[1] *Westminster Review*, April, 1877.

indictment against a whole race drawn by an ama-
teur philanthropist who only saw portions of the
people in one corner of the continent where, by
his own account, they are so harassed by the slave-
traders that progress is impossible. . . . So the
Reviewer, continuing, makes a disparaging inference as to the character and capacity of all Africans from the want of success that has attended
the efforts of the so-called negro communities in
Christian lands, who under the government of the
Europeans show no marked ability ; or who, as in
the case of Hayti and Liberia, have set up for
themselves, as alleged, ill-contrived, unstable, or
unsuitable governments. . . . These negroes,
as far as they are purely Africans, do not represent
even the average intellectual or moral qualities of
the African at home." [1]

A proper understanding of at least the fact
of such racial distinctions is necessary in order
to comprehend, not simply the question concerning Mohammedanism in Africa, but as well
the whole problem of the continent. Prof.
F. Max Müller [2] presents Waitz's classification,
which seems to be in general the division of the
races accepted now. One important modification, however, is to be made, in that the Nubian

[1] Blyden, *Christianity, Islam, and the Negro Race*, 308, 312.
[2] *The Origin and Growth of Religion*, 66.

and the Fulah races, separated by Waitz, are united into one group by later ethnologists. This general division seems to have been elaborated by Messrs. Cust and Ravenstein—founded upon linguistic indications—and has been indicated in a language and racial map of Africa.[1] According to this scheme we have :

I.   The Hamitic races—in three groups: (a) Egyptian—including the Copts, (b) Berber, (c) Ethiopic.

Of these three subdivisions, the Berbers are the ones with whom we have chiefly to deal in studying Mohammedanism in Africa ; for the Mohammedanism of Egypt is distinctly Turkish or Arabian, rather than African. Although the Berbers have been largely tinctured by direct contact with modern Turkish Mohammedanism, yet they are as a race so distinctly and so sufficiently African as to help us to understand what Mohammedanism in Africa is.

The present home of the Berber race is chiefly in the Barbary States, along the northern coast of Africa. The race is now largely

[1] Reproduced in the *Church Missionary Atlas*, i., Africa. London, 1887.

mixed with Arab and negro and Turkish elements. The civilisation of Morocco, Algiers,
Tunis, and Tripoli is now diversified by French
and Turkish and English interests so largely as
to be unrecognisable in many places ; but in
the interior, through so much of the great
northern desert as is still under the control of
this family of the native population, life and
religion are still as they have been for a long
time past, and as they will be for some time
to come.

The Barbary towns were long ago described.[1]
Later information simply confirms earlier statements — the darkness has been deepening.
" Such is the delusion of all these seacoast
Barbary towns : at a distance and without,
beauty and brilliancy ; but near and within,
filth and wretchedness." Even the country of
Morocco, looked upon by the faithful Mohammedans as to be held next to Arabia in reverent
estimation, is so abominably governed by its
Sultan and in many ways comes into question
with the great European Powers which it ap-

---

[1] *Travels in the Great Desert of Sahara*, James Richardson,
London, 1848.

proaches so closely in position, that a partition
is called for, in order that European control,
superseding the so-called civilisation of the
Mohammedan, may protect interests native as
well as foreign.

Most of the coast-line of northern Africa
is in the hands of the Arab element of the
population ; to find the real Berber civilisation, one must pass to the interior, into the
Desert of Sahara, and study the tribes of the
great Touarik family. Few travellers have had
much to do with this large and important company of tribes. Yet they rule over many thousands of miles in that desert region which is
their home. Mr. James Richardson, a corre-
spondent of one of the London newspapers, in
the years 1845, 1846, made a venturesome journey into their country—being almost, or quite,
the only one who up to that time had been able
to penetrate that region and to return with
his story. He describes a civilisation simple,
but in many respects admirable. Untamed
sons of the desert, they still hold themselves in admirable restraint, so far as the
great and common laws of morality are con-

cerned. He travelled a long time among them,
and met with little indication of savagery
and sensuality, though it must be confessed
that their religious fanaticism rendered his position at times difficult. He points out, however,
indications of a decided retrogression in the
material prosperity of that region. Thus:
"Formerly Fezzan was exceedingly rich and
populous, but now it has become impoverished
to the last degree, and many of its largest district populations are reduced to the starvation
point." Throughout, many hints are given of
oases being encroached upon by the desert,
of the inhabitants being under the greatest
stress for support, of apparent decrease in both
population and prosperity. "The process which
has reduced so many once populous cities and
villages to deserts, and left large portions of
the Barbary States with only the mouldering
ruins of their former greatness, has been a
gradual one."[1] It may be that the recent advance of European interests throughout North
Africa has of late stimulated somewhat the civ-

[1] *Oriental Religions and Christianity*, F. F. Ellinwood,
D.D., 201.

ilisation of this region. But we have gained this fact of importance, viz., that in the Berber element of the Mohammedan population of Africa we have a race strong, capable, comparatively elevated, tenacious, and important.

II. Turn now to the Semitic element. This is composed largely of the Arabs—called Moors along the northern edge of the continent. Apart from the Berbers, and excepting a large protuberance of the purely negro population north of Lake Tchad, the whole of North Africa from fifteen degrees latitude may be said to be populated by the Arab race. Throughout the desert region, particularly the western part of Sahara and the region immediately west of the river Nile, they are supreme. In the interior of Equatorial Africa, from fifteen degrees latitude south to fifteen degrees north, there are Arab stations and settlements,—" sparsely scattered, inhabited by but few Arabs with their retainers, powerful only by comparison with the utter feebleness of native powers around, useful as bases of operation and cities of refuge for the slave-hunters during their expeditions into the interior."

" A considerable portion of those who make Central Africa their home are the riff-raff of the Arabic nation, and largely responsible for the ill-odour in which the Arab is held in the interior. Yet whenever you come across him, whether at the coast or in the remotest deserts, you usually find in him the same courteous manner, and the same readiness to entertain strangers with his always polite, somewhat superficial, but none the less agreeable hospitality. The Englishman, who is himself troubled little by manners in his own country, will find himself much at a disadvantage in dealing with the polished, dignified Arab, even in the wilds of Central Africa." [1]

The Arabs are, largely, the merchants and the slave-traders of Central and Northern Africa. Thus: " The only trade of any importance carried on with Uganda, is entirely in the hands of the Arabs and half-breed merchants from Zanzibar." [2] Dr. Pruen gives an interesting illustration of their character, as well as business methods and capability, in the statement which he makes, that he had, far in the interior, paid these Arabs for goods " with

[1] *The Arab and the African*, S. T. Pruen, 254.
[2] *Uganda and the Egyptian Soudan*, Messrs. Wilson and Felkin, i., 189.

an English cheque which they at once accepted
at the value which I told them it represented " [1]
He seems to have studied accurately these
men, as he thus describes them : [2]

" Perhaps, to a popularly opposite view of the
case, I must protest against the right of the Arabs
as such to be in any way entitled a religious nation. Had the Mohammedan scheme been en-
trusted to Arab keeping alone ; had not Persian,
Mongol, Turkish, nay, at times European influences and races come to its aid, few would have
been ere this the readers of the Koran, and the
fasters of Ramadan. . . . A strong love and a
high appreciation of national and personal liberty,
a hatred of minute interference and special regula-
tions, a great respect for authority so long as it is
decently well exercised, joined with a remarkable
freedom from anything like caste-feeling in what
concerns ruling families and dynasties, much
practical good sense, much love of commercial
enterprise, a great readiness to undertake long
journeys and voluntary expatriation by land and
sea in search of gain and power, patience to endure,
and perseverance in the employment of means to
ends, courage in war, vigour in peace, and, lastly,
the marked predominance of a superior race over
whomever they came in contact with among their

[1] *The Arab and the African*, S. T. Pruen, 256.
[2] *Ibid.*, 261, 262.

Asiatic or African neighbours, a superiority admitted
by these last as a matter of course and an acknow-
leged right. . . . The Arab completely released
from the curse of Islam, which does more harm by
standing in the way of his development than by
actually corrupting him, would be a really fine
character ; and he is so thoroughly fitted, physi-
cally, intellectually, and socially, for work in the
interior of Africa, that if he could but be brought
to the saving knowledge of Christ, the difficult
question of the evangelisation of the Dark Continent would practically be solved."

But let us not idealise too largely the Arabs
of Africa—the slavers, the robbers, the desolat-
ors of a continent.

III. We have next the Nuba-Fulah group
—evidently an ancient race, aboriginal in the
lower basin of the Nile.[1] Light brown in colour ; a powerful, superior race ; quite distinct
from the Egyptian on the one side and the
negro on the other. Some of their tribes, as
the Massai, are considered of the most savage
peoples in East Africa. The Nyamnyam tribe
belongs to this family—as described by Schweinfurth in his *Heart of Africa*. The great Hausa

[1] *Encyclopedia of Missions*, ii., 186.

tribe is of this class, with its advanced civilisation :

" fast-walled cities of fifty, eighty, and even one hundred thousand inhabitants ; caravans are always streaming out — to the south to raid for slaves, and to the North African states across the Sahara to sell. Weavers, dyers, and shoemakers work hard in the streets of these great cities, manufacturing ample clothing that the people wear, and exhibit this remarkable spectacle of African civilisation." [1]

They are largely or entirely Mohammedans— at least in name ; "they dominate as Mohammedan foreign conquerors ; they cultivate Mohammedan learning with much enthusiasm ; they are numerous and powerful." [2] We have in this a race markedly superior and capable, particularly in Western and Central Soudan.

IV. The Negro. This is the race from which, largely, the general idea of African population has been derived. For from this race have the slaves principally been taken. Their home is along the West Coast for fifteen degrees north of the equator. This is the race that bears the

[1] *The Church at Home and Abroad*, vii., 507.
[2] *Encyclopedia of Missions*, ii., 186.

characteristics, physical, mental, and moral, that distinguish so emphatically the black man. It has been supposed that all Africa is inhabited by this race; hence the Africans throughout were judged in accordance with the former slave population of America,—the projecting jaw, small brain cavity, flat nose, protruding lips, thick skull, projecting heel, black and odorous skin, short and woolly hair. Somewhat inferior in mental development; naturally gentle, sunny, and childlike; easily influenced; indolent, improvident, contented. There is some little development in the arts of life; Mungo Park describes the capital, Bambasi, a city of thirty thousand people with two-story houses—though this may have been partly Mohammedan rather than negro civilisation. Evidently the country is thickly settled, dotted over with numerous towns inhabited by varying numbers up to 150,000 souls.[1] We have enough to indicate an interesting if not advanced race.

V. The Bantu or Zulu or Kafir race. This is the family of tribes concerning which most

[1] *The Independent*, xlv., 504.

has been written in the works of the later African travellers. Originally, as is supposed, they came from Western Asia. There are probably more than fifty millions of this race in Africa— a quarter of the whole population. This race has developed a wonderful language, giving thereby indication of large possibility in the line of civilisation. In person they are finer-looking than the negro, and are separated from the latter in that they speak a totally different language. The descriptions given of them by travellers are full of surprise and interest. Thus the social order shown in Uganda, one of the northernmost of the Bantu kingdoms, is almost startling; evidently the Bantus are capable of a high civilisation. Livingstone, Colenso, and Wilberforce thought them " the counterpart of our civilisation." [1] Mr. Mackay, missionary in Uganda, bore witness to the fact that some of his scholars seemed quite to comprehend the argument in the seventh, eighth, and ninth chapters of Romans which would indicate intellectual ability above that of many of our own fellow countrymen. The race is decidedly

[1] *The Church at Home and Abroad*, xii., 404.

musical.[1] The beautiful faithfulness with which
the Bantu servants of Livingstone carried and
cared for the dead body of their master until
they had brought it to the sea is one of the
most touching stories of the kind in all literature. The good qualities of the Congo tribes
are testified to by many travellers; there is a
vitality of grace and power about the Bantu
that will make him take his place some day
among the nations of the earth.[2] Mr. Arnot
travelled through the Bantu country " without
bodyguard or arms, without companions white
or black." " Repeatedly the natives expressed
their joy and satisfaction at the way I had
treated them by coming amongst them with
' open hands.' "[3] To Henry M. Stanley, the
Wahuma race brought up thoughts of " those
blameless people with whom the gods deign to
banquet once a year upon the heights of
Ethiopia."[4] Professor Drummond's repetition
of the usual traveller's estimate of the depraved

[1] *Story of Uganda*, by S. G. Stock, i., 149 ; *The Arab and
the African*, S. T. Pruen, 99–105.
[2] *The Missionary Review of the World*, ii., 132.
[3] *The Church at Home and Abroad*, vi., 65.
[4] *The Missionary Review of the World*, iv., 294.

Zanzibaris is contradicted by Dr. Pruen ; who says that they are " as a rule surprisingly honest, kind-hearted, and faithful." [1]   This is the more surprising in that, of all African tribes, the Bantus of Zanzibar have been perhaps under the worst influences. Testimony almost without end might be adduced to support the statement that in this great Bantu family we have a magnificent race of men, with grand possibilities for future civilisation.

VI. The sixth class of inhabitants is the Hottentot family—the lowest in the scale of humanity in Africa. It includes as well the pygmy tribes lately discovered. As Mohammedanism has had little or no contact with this family of men it is not necessary, for our purpose now, to describe them. The inhabitants of the island of Madagascar are of still another and distinct race—being allied to the Malay family. They also do not come into our line of thought at this time.

In general, and concerning all the different races thus suggested, it is evident that Mohammedanism in Africa has to deal with races of

[1] *The Arab and the African*, S. T. Pruen, 98.

men capable of much. The wild and impossible African is largely a creature of the imagination. The contempt that the white races have felt toward the black races is hardly justified, so far at least as many of these African tribes are concerned. Some one has said, "The fate of the negro is the romance of our age"; it has been, rather, a tragedy thus far. Before European civilisation can make much progress with the African this fundamental fact must be realised—that we have men, capable races of men, with whom to deal. It is because the Arab has recognised this fact more largely than the European, that he has made himself so effective, for bad or good, throughout the continent. The white man must recognise the manhood of the black man. Intellectually he is capable; there is no truth which the negro is unable to grasp.[1] Livingstone's profound observation concerning them was that "goodness impresses them."[2] There is not a tribe on the continent of Africa that does not stretch out its hands to the great Creator, that does not

[1] *The Missionary Review of the World*, i., 98.
[2] *Garenganze*, Arnot, 266.

recognise the Supreme Being." [1]   Fetichism,
witchcraft, reign supreme and drag into lifelong
fear ; but behind and above all is a vague
theism.   The negro is far different from the
Caucasian ; but that he is not essentially inferior is a thought that we need to learn.   Intertribal war has destroyed all possibility of
accumulation and consequent civilisation ; an
innate instability of character has, to some degree, been developed [2]; stupidity, according to
Western ideas, characterises many of the tribes [3];
an extraordinary indifference to the future may
be noted [4]; fear of hunger and fear of punish-
ment are the two great motives that control. [5]
But the African is a man.

[1] Blyden, *Christianity, Islam, and the Negro Race*, 132.
[2] *The Arab and the African*, S. T. Pruen, 309.
[3] *Ibid.*, 276.
[4] *Ibid.*, 265 · Blyden, *Christianity, Islam, and the Negro
Race*, 308.
[5] *The Arab and the African*, S. T. Pruen, 242.

CHAPTER V

THE MOHAMMEDAN CONQUEST OF AFRICA

WITHIN one hundred years after the flight of Mohammed from Mecca, the Hejira, the empire of his successors extended from India to the Atlantic Ocean, over " the various and distant provinces which may be known under the names of Persia, Syria, Egypt, Africa, and Spain.[1] Startling advance ; taking everything into consideration, incomparable in the history of the race. Of these magnificent conquests but one comes into our consideration now—Africa.

We are told that Mohammed regarded Africa with peculiar interest and affection. At one time, when his followers were sorely persecuted in Arabia, he devised an asylum in Africa: "Yonder lieth a country wherein no man is wronged—a land of righteousness. Depart

[1] Gibbon, *Roman Empire*, vi., 289.

thither, and remain until it pleaseth the Lord
to open your way before you." [1]   Events took
such a turn that the prophet was enabled to
make for his followers a home and throne in his
own land ; but into the region of the "Ethi-
opians" his followers later made entrance as
conquerors.   Far beyond the imagination of
the prophet, Africa has proved itself a fruitful
home for Islam.

It is necessary for us to remind ourselves of
the condition of North Africa in the times
immediately preceding the advent of Islam.
Christianity ruled in the land, but "wofully
weakened and rent by wild heresies and
schisms." [2]   Mighty fathers of the Church had
found a home, had done work, throughout that
region—Tertullian, Origen, Cyprian, Augustine,
and many others.   It is said that there were
four or five hundred bishops—which means,
of course, thousands of churches and priests—
in North Africa at that time. [3]   But the early
purity of the Christian faith had been, during

---

[1] Blyden, *Christianity, Islam, and the Negro Race*, 266.

[2] *Oriental Religions and Christianity*, F. F. Ellinwood,
D.D , 201.

[3] *Report of Missionary Conference*, London, 1888, i., 29.

those six centuries, largely lost through strife and division. Heresy and ambition had greatly weakened the Church. The decadence of Roman ecclesiastical and civil authority was sadly evident ; there was little or no solidarity in the communities of North Africa. The social structure there was like the card houses which children build,—when Islam touched Egypt, the whole edifice fell. It is claimed by a somewhat enthusiastic admirer of Mohammedanism "that the form of Christianity which it supplanted in North Africa . . . was infinitely inferior to Mohammedanism itself." [1] But unless Islam has terribly degenerated, it is hard to see how any mediæval form of Christianity, however debased, could have been "inferior" to the unspeakable degradation of things social, commercial, and religious in those lands now—except so far as European influence of late has modified matters. With the irresistible enthusiasm of a new-born faith, Islam advanced against, and over, a divided and helpless community, largely Christian—and left behind something worse, not better.

[1] *Mohammed and Mohammedanism*, Bosworth Smith, 228.

The progress of Islam over Northern Africa
was like that of a blazing prairie fire—rapid,
scorching, desolating. And yet Christianity
struggled desperately. We are told that fourteen times it was driven by the sword into
apostasy, and fourteen times it returned to its
ancient faith. In spite of the banishment to
the deserts of Arabia of multitudes of men of
all ranks, in spite of solicitations, seductions,
caresses, the Catholic Church remained stead-
fast at its post at Carthage and in Tunis proper
for more than six centuries after the Mussulman's conquest.[1] For sixty years North Africa
wrestled with the Mohammedan warriors. The
Christians and the pagan Moors united in
opposition. But, though they could hinder,
they could not stop the victorious advance of
Abdallah and Zobeir, but particularly of Akbah,
justly called the " Conqueror of Africa." Under
these leaders, especially the last, the deserts of
North Africa were traversed almost as if civilisation and abundance welcomed the conquerors on every side. They penetrated to the

---

[1] Quoted by Dr. Blyden, from a Bull of Pope Leo XIII.,
in *Christianity, Islam, and the Negro Race*, 353.

Atlantic coast. Akbah spurred his horse into the waves and, raising his eyes to heaven, exclaimed with the cry of a true fanatic: "Great God! if my course were not stopped by this sea, I would still go on to the unknown kingdom of the West, preaching the unity of Thy holy name, and putting to the sword the rebellious nations who worship any other gods than Thee."[1] Gradually the Christian population was overwhelmed; slowly the Moors, or Berbers, were converted to the Mohammedan faith and allegiance. The Arabs that had come from Asia through Egypt into the northern desert were gradually merged with the Berber race that was closely akin; the remnants of other races there present were slowly absorbed; until all coalesced under the banner of Islam, unitedly turning their faces towards Mecca.

In the early days of that fierce struggle there arose a negro statesman and warrior, Soni Heli Ischia, who created a vast negro empire; in opposition to the Moors, who sought to extend the political supremacy of Islam from the north, even in those early days, down into

[1] Gibbon, *Roman Empire*, vi., 348.

the region south of the Saharan desert. This negro patriot is said to have obtained control from Timbuctoo westward to the Atlantic and eastward to Abyssinia, a line of about three thousand miles in length.[1] If what is stated be historic, it gives us an instructive hint of the Central African in those days, and of possibilities in the future.

It would be needless, whether or not possible, to follow the progress of that early conquest, step by step. Gradually Mohammedanism obtained control of the various tribes. On the whole a steady progress in conversion, but not in civilisation, has been made throughout the centuries, reaching its climax in the awful rule of the Mahdi, and his successor the Khalifa.

" This vast expanse of country has now fallen into an almost indescribable state of moral and religious decadence. In the Sudan, we have before us a terrible example of a nascent and somewhat crude civilisation suddenly shattered by wild, ignorant, and almost savage tribes who have built over the scattered remnants a form of government based, to some extent, on the lines they found existing, but from which they have eradicated almost

[1] Blyden, *Christianity, Islam, and the Negro Race,* 141.

every symbol of right, justice and morality, and for which they have substituted a rule of injustice, ruthless barbarity, and immorality. Nor can I recall any other instance in modern times of a country in which a semblance of civilisation has existed for upwards of half a century, falling back into a state so little removed from absolute barbarism." [1]

With continued fanaticism there has been a gradual advance through the north of Africa of that process of desolation which has brought a once flourishing region into desert-like isolation, into poverty and degradation. Mohammedanism in North Africa is well indicated by the desert mosques which Mr. Richardson found in his travels through the Saharan desert— simply an outline, in small stones, of the ground-plan of Mohammedan temples. Here the devout passers-by "occasionally stopped and prayed." [2] Unbuilt, uncovered, unsurrounded by habitation—the spirit of prayer therein offered, the heat of fanaticism therein shown, is only equalled by the utter desolation of the prayer-place under the heat of the Saharan sun.

[1] *Fire and Sword in the Sudan*, Slatin Pasha, 622.
[2] *Travels in the Great Desert of Sahara*, James Richardson, London, 1848, ii., 269.

For centuries the countries along the northern shore of Africa have been under the control
of Mohammedanism, and we have hinted at
the desolating effects.   Gradually progress has
been made southward through the desert and
into North-Central Africa.   But only lately
has Mohammedanism been carried with conquering power into Central Africa.   In our
own days its merchant missionaries, largely
slavers, have been pacing pathways throughout
Central and even into South-Central Africa as
far south as fifteen degrees below the equator.
The story of this recent Mohammedan advance
is wonderful, the conquest of a little world
within this century! Few realise what the
progress has been.

It is in comparatively recent times that the
Arabs took possession of the eastern coast
around Zanzibar, and of the interior from there.
They sailed from Arabia and threw themselves
upon the eastern African coast, dispossessing
the inert Portuguese who had held these regions
with more or less of control since the time of
Vasco Da Gama in the early part of the six-
teenth century.   Persistently, rapidly, Moham-

medan agents made progress throughout the interior, establishing small settlements, proselyting among the natives, obtaining political control, and terrorising throughout. Their scorching presence has been manifested as far south as Mozambique and throughout the Lake Nyassa region. Through the past few decades they have been wandering, with but little hindrance, from the extreme north thus far through the south—and from the east through to the west. With them, markedly, business and religion have been identified. Mr. Richardson in his travels through the Great Desert, found that the merchants of Ghadames " often remain in Soudan five, ten, even fifteen and twenty years, leaving their families here whilst they accumulate a fortune in commercial speculations. Sometimes they marry other wives in Soudan and form another establishment." [1] There is a something characteristic of Mohammedanism in the desire for wife and home which these Arabs develop; marrying the one, and creating the other, wherever they go for a

[1] *Travels in the Great Desert of Sahara*, James Richardson, London, 1848, i., 98.

while.   Again he testifies,[1] "I see in them the
mixture of a religious and commercial character
blended in a most extraordinary manner and degree."   Slaves are their chief business concern,
with all the unspeakable horrors of the traffic.
Arab traders are among the chief importers of
the intoxicating spirits which are degrading
Africa.[2]   Ivory and the slave-trade go together ;
the slaves are purchased or captured to carry the
ivory from the inland to the coast ; and both
are sold on arriving at the destination.   Shrewd,
selfish, successful traders are these Arabs, blight-
ing a continent to gratify their greed.

But what interests us particularly at this time
is the way in which Mohammedanism has been,
by these means, advanced throughout the northern and central regions of the continent.   Its
progress is in general due either to force or
fraud, or both.   This is the method.[3]   Let us
suppose a region of one hundred large villages ;
forty of them become Moslem, and are unmo-
lested ; sixty are raided, captured, or destroyed.

[1] *Travels in the Great Desert of Sahara*, James Richardson,
London, 1848, i., 383.
[2] *The Missionary Review of the World*, i., 99.
[3] *Ibid.*, i., 865.

That region is now reported as converted. Long after, because of the memories of the natives that survive, the Arab master will be obeyed, and the Arab religion will be in form observed—so far as immunity is promised thereby. The story of Tippu Tib, Mr. Stanley's "friend," if such he can be called, well illustrates the conquest of Central Africa by Mohammed-anism. He had been a coast slaver. By a fortunate raid he got possession of a large amount of ivory and many slaves. Successful disposal of this booty enabled him to obtain guns and war slaves. He continued a tri-umphant, unchecked course from the south of Tanganyika northwards towards what is now known as the Congo Free State : he ravaged on every side, gathering ivory and making slaves by hundreds. He learned from a captive that the king of a district not far off had disap-peared mysteriously many years before, and that the people were waiting for him to return, or for some legitimate successor to claim au-thority. Tippu Tib artfully conceived the plan of representing himself as the son and heir, and accordingly schooled himself in all the local

knowledge necessary for the deception he intended to practise. By the time he reached
that region he could rehearse the long lines of
the king's ancestry, the names of his living
relatives and the elders of the land ; and was
familiar with the events, traditions, and customs
of the country. He despatched messengers
into the country to announce his arrival, and
to tell the wondering people the news of his
father's fate, and of his intention to assume his
father's rights. The people accepted the story
without difficulty, and offered to escort him
with honour to his father's land—which, as
Mr. Stanley humorously relates, Tippu Tib
courteously accepted. On arrival, he told the
chiefs the story of his father's disappearance,
with a wealth of fictitious details. They were
thoroughly persuaded that he was no other
than their lost king's son ; and he was formally
installed as their king. Before many days had
passed, the people of the region were made to
understand that ivory was very acceptable to
their king; and heaps of it were daily laid
before him. Finally, when he had depleted
the region of ivory, he sought occasion to

embroil this kingdom with the neighbouring
tribes, which gave him opportunity to despatch
his native force for the purpose of despoiling
the surrounding regions. Within fifteen months
he had gathered nine hundred tusks; and he
now proposed to his admiring subjects that
they should muster carriers to convey his treas-
ures to another country which he said he owned.
Thus he brought his ivory to the market; and
the Arabs of the region "hailed him as genius
and recognised his superiority." The almost
infinite cruelty of the whole process can be,
however, but faintly imagined. It is said that
he realised one hundred and fifty thousand
dollars by the sale of this accumulation.[1] In
1890 he commanded on the Upper Congo,
authority unchallenged, with an army of two
thousand men provided with Winchester rifles.[2]
He, and such as he, carry Mohammedanism
with them as they go, and represent it to the
native tribes.

It is hard to draw a dividing line between
the raiding of Mohammedan slave-dealers and

[1] *Slavery and the Slave Trade in Africa*, H. M. Stanley,
29–34. [2] *The Missionary Review of the World*, iii., 470.

the establishment of Mohammedanism as a religion in Central Africa. The former is legiti-
mately a shading off of the latter. We may
presume that as distance and time have weakened Mohammedan enthusiasm, the outreach-
ing towards the south from the Mohammedan
kingdoms in North-Central Africa has been
more and more largely that purely selfish interest which is involved in the trade element of
their religion ; and perhaps the conquest of
Zanzibar by the Arabs, and their approach into
the interior from that coast, has been almost
entirely for the purpose of trade and with little
thought of proselytism. And yet the story of
Uganda indicates clearly that even the slave-
traders seek to advance their religion politically,
whether or not for purely selfish purposes. We
must, however, see clearly that there has been,
particularly in North-Central Africa, an advance
of Mohammedanism that is akin in enthusiasm
and startling success to the early conquest of
the northern border of the continent. Thus " a
cordon of Mohammedan states " has been created along the southern edge of the desert.
The Mohammedan kingdom of Sokoto contains

"vast walled cities of fifty and eighty and even one hundred thousand inhabitants, out of which caravans are always streaming—to the south to raid for slaves, to the North-African states across the Sahara to sell them."[1] South of this district dwell largely the Hausas, a splendid race of men of whom we have already made mention. It is said that there are fifteen millions of them; they have recently adopted the Mohammedan rites.[2] Fifty years ago Mr. Richardson[3] described the fanaticism and success with which the Fulah races, under the influence of Mohammedanism, had during the preceding forty years, more or less, arisen to fame and power. From mere Arab wanderers they had become, by intermixing with the negroes in a career of enlarging conquest and settlement, the leading people along the south-western edge of the Great Desert. "Their progress has been the main cause of the great spread of Islam in West Africa in the present century."[4] The Mohammedanism of the Hau-

[1] *The Church at Home and Abroad*, vii., 505. [2] *Ibid.*, 505.
[3] *Travels in the Great Desert of Sahara*, James Richardson, London, 1848, i., 303.
[4] *Church Missionary Atlas*, i., 38.

sas and the Fulahs now holds that whole vast region in allegiance to the great prophet. And their fanaticism does not seem, as yet, to have exhausted itself. It is largely throughout the regions immediately south of these two peoples, apparently, that Mohammedanism has lately been making real conquest—religious accession as distinguished from mere slave-raiding. Dr. Blyden asserts that a quiet, non-militant progress has been going on throughout that region; and he is corroborated by the assertion of Prof. Crummell that "Mohammedanism is rapidly and peaceably spreading all through the tribes of Western Africa."[1] Also, the Rev. James Johnson, possibly a better authority on the matter than either of the preceding two, has asserted that "three-fourths of the additions to Mohammedanism in the region about Sierra Leone are from conviction and not by natural increase by birthright "[2]; though Bishop Crowther would modify this statement.[3] We seem warranted in asserting that there has been

[1] Blyden, *Christianity, Islam, and the Negro Race,* 199, 202.
[2] *The Missionary Review of the World,* i., 381.
[3] *The Church at Home and Abroad,* iii., 594.

actual and successful proselytism by Islam throughout large regions in the western part of North-Central Africa, extending far towards the east in the great Soudan. Dr. Blyden asserts that Mohammedanism has gained control of the most energetic and enterprising tribes in Africa.

"It has built and occupies the largest cities in the heart of the continent ; its laws regulate the most powerful kingdoms, it is daily gaining converts from the ranks of paganism, and it commands respect among all Africans wherever it is known, even where the people have not submitted to the sway of the Koran." [1]

But such statements may easily give rise to false inferences ; they must be interpreted and limited by what we have said before.

Indeed we cannot help thinking that there is much exaggeration concerning Mohammedan control and advance in Africa.   Thus Dr. Blyden asserts [2]: " One-half of the whole continent is dominated by Islam ; while of the remaining half, one-quarter is leavened by it and the other one-quarter is threatened by it."   Again [3]:

[1] Blyden, *Christianity, Islam, and the Negro Race*, 6, 7.
[2] *The Church at Home and Abroad*, vii., 409.
[3] Blyden, *Christianity, Islam, and the Negro Race*, preface x.

" Mohammedanism, by its simple, rigid forms
of worship, by its literature, its politics, its organised society, its industry and commercial
activities, is rapidly superseding a hoary and
pernicious paganism." A general impression
has been created by these and similar statements to the effect that, as Islam conquered
North Africa in the seventh century, so now it
is conquering Central and Southern Africa in
the nineteenth century. But no statement
could well be farther from the truth. Even
the assumption that slave-raiding is religious
conquest will not verify such an assertion. The
fact seems to be that south of the line of the
Mohammedan states, from the twentieth to the
tenth parallels of latitude north of the equator,
Mohammedan control is largely a mercantile
supremacy, established by fire-arms, involving
considerable political management of native
heathen tribes. Such as it is, Mohammedanism has nearly reached its limit of expansion in
Africa.[1] Its control, if such it can be called,
will readily be overthrown with the crushing of
the Arab slave power—a process rapidly being

[1] *The Missionary Review of the World*, i., 97.

accomplished. Already the Arabs have been checked, if not checkmated, in the Congo Free State. The desperate efforts that they have made to establish control in the Nyassa region seem to have been fully overcome. In the revolutions and counter-revolutions in the important kingdom of Uganda, apparently, Mohammedanism as represented by the Arab traders has been defeated. The crushing defeat of the Khalifa by General Kitchener in September, 1898, seems a death-blow. The recent advance of Mohammedanism in Africa has reached its limit; with the full destruction of the Arab slave-trader, the advance of Islam will cease.

CHAPTER VI

ITS MISSIONARY CHARACTER

MOHAMMEDANISM is one of the great missionary religions of the world, though its motives and methods are largely low. Its career throughout has been one of proselytism through conquest. In this it contrasts markedly with Christianity; for the religion of Jesus Christ has made a career rather of conquest through proselytism. But Christianity and Mohammedanism are the two great missionary religions of the world. Buddhism for a while went forth conquering and to conquer; but its missionary spirit has exhausted itself and is not an essential characteristic of the religion. It has been well remarked: "When a religion loses its missionary spirit it dies." It is because Mohammedanism is so essentially a missionary religion that it has so magnificently conquered; and it is because that missionary spirit has been revived, and is fervent, in Africa during this century that we have to meet the great problems contained in our subject. Here has been one of the greatest outbreaks of missionary zeal that human history presents—but on the part of Mohammedanism rather than Christianity.

There are certain fundamental principles of Islam which necessitate this missionary effort, and make success comparatively easy. Thus, it is ingrained in the very constitution of the true believer that he is to go out to the infidel; he is not to wait for the infidel to come to him. The claims of Mohammed were emphatic; his follower was under obligation to force them upon the world around, and the infidel was under obligation to recognise and believe. If the unbeliever should refuse, then came the forced choice—" Believe, pay tribute, or die." As with resistless enthusiasm the early followers of the prophet swept like " the pestilence that walketh in darkness and the destruction that wasteth at noon-day " over the world, as they held the drawn scimitar over the necks of prostrate nations, we can hardly wonder that large masses of men accepted the first of these possibilities, and consented to believe. There was business shrewdness, amounting almost to genius, in the proposal of the second of these choices —pay tribute; for, after all that may be said to the contrary, we must acknowledge that, with many, religious principle and love of life are more precious than gold; and many there were of those times who would pay tribute rather than believe or die.

Thus the Mohammedan went forth; but we must notice what an astonishingly simple creed he presented for belief. Simply say, " There is but one God and Mohammed is His prophet," simply perform a few necessary acts, and you are a Mohammedan, safe here and hereafter. That this statement is not exaggerated, is amply proved on every side. Mr. Richardson in his travels through the most fanatical Moslem tribes of the desert was constantly enjoined to confess himself as of Islam—simply by the recognition of Mohammed as the prophet of God. Security was assured to him if he would do this. Some few other travellers, notably

Caille, purchased security at the price of this profanation. It is easy to confess with the lips that Mohammed is the prophet of God, it is hard to pay tribute, it is bitterness extreme, even for a negro, to die ; can we wonder at the choice often made?

One other consideration explains the ease with which Islam has proselytised, especially in Africa : the recognition of equal manhood in all believers which Mohammed earnestly impressed upon his followers. Apparently there is no religion, Christianity not excepted, which gives such practical illustration of the essential equality of all fellow believers, whether white or black, bond or free. Theoretically, Christianity presents even a higher basis of equality, in that all true believers are sons of God ; but as things are at present, undoubtedly Mohammedanism, wherever its early enthusiasm still has sway, more completely obliterates false distinctions between man and man and uncovers the essential equality of believers. This principle is of especial avail in connection with the advance of Islam in Africa. For most of the nations of the Dark Continent seem pecu-

liarly susceptible to the impression made by
a stronger man, or nation, upon themselves.
The white man is readily recognised as superior, at least throughout a large part of Africa ;
and the Arab with his rifle, his fighting slaves,
his cruelty, is feared by the natives as one
above themselves. Now when the superior
being receives the native into something like
equality, simply on the basis of Mohammedan
belief, it makes the pagan more strongly in
favour of that religion. Mohammedanism tends
to break down tribal and caste distinctions. It
imbues the negro believer with a sense of dignity. It has been remarked that " the negro
who accepts Mohammedanism acquires at once
a sense of the dignity of human nature." [1]
Once a believer, there is nothing in his colour or
race to debar him from the highest privileges,
social or political, to which any other Moslem
can attain.[2] Said Mohammed to his followers,
" I admonish you to fear God and yield obedience to my successor, although he may be a
black slave." [3] And the Mahdi said to his slave
Slatin, " In the place of worship we are all alike."

---

[1] Quoted by Dr. Blyden, *Christianity, Islam, and the Negro
Race*, 11.   [2] *Ibid.*, 18.   [3] *Ibid.*, 281.

Here is a combination of mighty influences at work to facilitate the conversion of Africa to Mohammedanism : The impelling need, felt by the true believer, to force his religion upon the infidel ; the simple nature of the creed presented ; the preference of many to believe rather than to pay tribute or to die, especially when belief raises one into assured equality ; and with this potent fact in addition, that the tribe accepting Islam is no longer subject to slave-raids. But this opens before us a question on which there has been much misapprehension.   Thus it has been said,[1] " The slave who becomes a Mohammedan is free."   On the contrary, the testimony throughout Africa is that surely there are slaves that are Mohammedans, whether or not converted in slavery; and apparently Mohammedans do make actual Mohammedans slaves. Mr. Richardson in his travels in the desert[2] speaks of the slaves in the town of Ghadames as "mostly devout if not fanatic Mussulmans." We are warranted in asserting that there is at

---

[1] Blyden, *Christianity, Islam, and the Negro Race*, 18.
[2] *Travels in the Great Desert of Sahara*, James Richardson, London, 1848, i., 195.

least a spirit of fraternity throughout Islam that
gives it tremendous advantage in Africa. Mohammedanism " does not abolish slavery, but it
does take away its sting "—so far as Mohammedans are concerned. " Equality of all men before
God was a principle which Mohammed everywhere maintained ; and which, taking as it did
all caste feeling from slavery, took away also its
chief sin." [1] Certainly Islam rises far above
that narrow prejudice against the negro which
characterises too largely the white Christians—
as illustrated by Dr. E. A. Freeman's statement,
" The law may declare the negro to be the
equal of the white man, but it cannot make
him his equal." Or in Mr. Thomas Carlyle's
assertion that " God has put a whip in the
hand of every white man to flog the negro." [2]
On the contrary, Mohammedan history abounds
with examples of distinguished negroes. Billal,
a slave, a black man, a favourite of Mohammed,
the first muezzin or caller to prayer, was once
addressed by the great prophet somewhat in

[1] *Mohammed and Mohammedanism*, R. Bosworth Smith, 203.
[2] Quoted by Dr. Blyden, *Christianity, Islam, and the Negro
Race*, 333, 337.

this way : " What shoes were those you wore last night ?   Verily, as I journeyed into Paradise and was mounting the stairs of God, I heard your footsteps before me, though I could not see."

Into three phrases we may condense the description and explanation of Mohammedan missionary advance in Africa—native agents, simple methods, intolerant zeal.

It is largely through native agency that Islam has been propagated in Africa.   For the Arabs that penetrate the interior, whether for good or ill, may now be called natives of the country.   They are recognised by the negro as in it, if not fully of it.   In the wide inclusiveness of the races to which we have already referred concerning Africa, the Arabs are now certainly of the native population.   Even the invaders of Zanzibar, a century ago, have made Africa their home and have identified themselves, though disastrously, with the native races. The difference between the white man and the Arab, in native estimation, shows clearly that the Arab is to be counted an as indigenous agent.

But Mohammedanism makes use of other agents, more closely allied to the negro, in securing its advance. Let us refer again to the Hausas and the Fulahs as perhaps the most conspicuous agents in the great advance of Mohammedanism throughout Western and Central Soudan. These magnificent tribes, one purely negro and the other mixed but now essentially native, have carried Mohammedanism through the forests, from the desert to the ocean in one direction, and to the lakes in the other.

Much has been said of late concerning the great University of Cairo as a training-school for native agents of Mohammedanism in Africa. Dr. Blyden quotes the following description of this great institution at Cairo—the educational pride and glory of Islam.

"This university is nine hundred years old (older than Oxford), and still flourishes with as much vigour as in the palmy days of the Arabian conquest. There I saw collected ten thousand students. As one expressed it 'there were two acres of turbans' assembled in a vast enclosure, with no floor but a pavement, and with a roof over it supported by four hundred columns, and at the foot of every column a teacher surrounded by his pupils. These students are from all parts of Africa. . . . When their studies are ended, those who are to be missionaries mount their camels, and, joining a caravan across the desert, are lost in the far interior of Africa." [1]

On the other hand, take the report of General Haig, sent out by the Church Missionary Society about the year 1887.[2] He makes an intelligent statement to the effect that he had never heard of missionaries being sent out from the college to spread the faith anywhere, and did not believe that there was any organisation for Central Africa. According to his statement, the number of students in the Ashar varies according to political events. Just before a great conscription, the number is enlarged with a view of avoiding the enlistment. Sometimes the number reaches eight thousand. Weighing testimony, taking into consideration the statements of various travellers and writers, we are forced to the conclusion that Dr. Blyden's assertions concerning this monumental institution in Cairo are greatly exaggerated—particularly

[1] Blyden, *Christianity, Islam, and the Negro Race*, 191.
[2] *The Church at Home and Abroad*, ii., 486.

with regard to the missionary work of its grad-
uates in Africa. A careful study of available
facts will, we are persuaded, lead to the conclusion that Mohammedan advance is not due
to a missionary propaganda such as we are accustomed to think of in connection with Christian work, and such as has been attributed on a
large scale to the Cairo University. Undoubtedly many native Africans attend that school
of the faith. Certainly Mohammedan educational effort, as we shall see, is made elsewhere
in Africa. There seems to be clear testimony
to the effect that Mohammedan teachers, of a
certain sort, roam through the land ; and doubtless they have some influence as missionaries.[1]
But the indigenous agency on which Mohammedanism principally depends is the power of
the native Mohammedan state, exerted mightily to conquer and thereby convert.

Accepting, however, the assertions that some
individuals go forth throughout many of the
pagan tribes and regions of Africa teaching
Mohammedanism,—though largely for purposes
of personal gain,—it is interesting to notice the

[1] Blyden, *Christianity, Islam, and the Negro Race*, 431.

simple methods which are pursued in making this advance.   Dr. Blyden's description of these Mohammedan missionaries is almost pathetic.

"In going from town to town, and village to village, they go simply as the bearers of God's truth. They take their mats or their skins, and their manuscripts, and are followed by their pupils, who in every new pagan town form the nucleus of a school and congregation.   These preachers are the receivers, not the dispensers, of charity." [1]

"The Arab missionaries whom we have met in the interior go about without 'purse or scrip' and disseminate their religion by quietly teaching the Koran.   The native missionaries—Mandingoes and Fulahs—unite with the propagation of their faith active trading.   Wherever they go they produce the impression that they are not preachers only, but traders—but, on the other hand, that they are not traders merely, but preachers.   And in this way, silently and almost unobtrusively, they are causing princes to become obedient disciples and zealous propagators of Islam.   Their converts as a general thing become Muslims from choice and conviction, and bring all the manliness of their former condition to the maintenance and support of their new creed." [2]

"Local institutions were not destroyed when

[1] Blyden, *Christianity, Islam, and the Negro Race*, 194.
[2] *Ibid.*, 13.

Arab influences were introduced. They only as-
sumed new forms and adapted themselves to the
new teachings. In all thriving Mohammedan communities in West and Central Africa, it may be
noticed that the Arab superstructure has been
superimposed on a permanent indigenous substruct-
ure ; so that what really took place, when the Arab
met the negro in his own home, was a healthy
amalgamation, and not an absorption or an undue
repression." [1]

"After the first conquests of the Muslims in
North Africa, their religion advanced southwards
into the continent, not by armies but by schools
and books and mosques ; by trade and inter-
marriage." [2]

And Mr. Bosworth Smith asserts concerning
Mohammedanism in Africa that " it has spread,
not by the sword, but by earnest and simple-
minded Arab missionaries."

We have already ventured to dissent from
some of these statements, so positively made
concerning Islam and its advance in Africa. In
connection with the political character of Mohammedanism in Africa, we shall attempt to
see this more clearly. Bishop Crowther says, [3]

---

[1] Blyden, *Christianity, Islam, and the Negro Race*, 356.
[2] *Ibid.*, 14.
[3] Quoted in *Oriental Religions and Christianity*, F. F. Ellinwood, D.D., 210.

" The real vocation of these so-called quiet apostles of the Koran is that of fetish peddlers " ;
and in view of exaggerations of statement that
we are compelled to acknowledge as made by
Dr. Blyden, Canon Taylor, and those who re-
assert their conclusions, we can only say that
the authority of Bishop Crowther is to be
trusted in any contradiction.   It seems evident
that the picture of Mohammedan missionaries,
just quoted, is, to some extent, poetic imagination.

After making all due allowance, we are left
with these simple facts : that indigenous agents
have been at work, particularly throughout
Western and Central Soudan, hardly in the
beautiful and self-denying way described ; rather
as men seeking self-support by means more or
less honourable, but carrying with them as they
go, teachings of Mohammedanism and the Koran.   They familiarise the pagan tribes with
Islam.   Doubtless they win some converts.
When compulsion comes through political
events, when the dreadful alternative is presented, " Mohammedanism or slavery," the
choice is made the more easy.   Another tribe

ranges itself nominally, and perhaps actually, under the name of the prophet of God.

In this missionary advance, the sword and preaching, the soldier and the missionary, the state and the individual, supplement each other. An intolerant zeal is shown. To some extent it is true that "in Africa is the most fanatical and proselytising portion of the Mussulman world, in its negro converts."[1]

Mr. Richardson, throughout the Sahara Desert, not only saw but felt the fierce fanaticism of the Mohammedanism of that region. Said a Touarik to him: "You are a Christian ; the people of Timbuctoo will kill you unless you confess Mohammed to be the prophet of God."[2] "To have said a word, or even to have breathed a syllable, of disrespect about Mohammedanism would have exposed me to have been torn to pieces by the Mohammedans."[3] "It is next to impossible to induce the Sahara Mohammedans to think favourably of Christianity."[4]

[1] *Eastern Church*, Dean Stanley, 259.
[2] *Travels in the Great Desert of Sahara*, James Richardson, London, 1848, i., 118.
[3] *Ibid.*, ii., 25.
[4] *Ibid.*, ii., 83.

Mr. Anderson, a negro of Liberia, made a journey to Musardu, the capital city of the western Mandingoes. In his description of this fine race of negroes, speaking of their missionary activity, he says [1]: " Their zeal for Islam has caused the name of Mohammed to be pronounced in this part of Africa, where it otherwise would never have been mentioned." Slatin Pasha, in order to retain the obedience of his soldiers against the rising Mahdism, thought that he had to become a convert to Islam. [2]

It is made evident by a consensus of testimony that in North Africa Mohammedanism is furiously fanatic ; extending to violent hatred of all who are not Mohammedans. In approaching Central Africa, we find this zeal gradually less intolerant—though burning fiercely enough to make the Mohammedan tribes and rulers desirous of impressing their religion upon neighbouring tribes. Even in Central Africa, the Mohammedan law threatens with death both the proselytised and proselytiser [3]; but this

[1] *Journey to Musardu*, 6.
[2] *Fire and Sword in the Sudan*, Slatin Pasha, 217.
[3] *Church at Home and Abroad*, vii., 507.

seems to be directed simply against renegades.
The zeal which animates the "earnest and sim-
ple-minded missionaries of Mohammedanism"
is sufficiently mixed with selfishness to make
them more tolerant than the furies of early
Mohammedan history, and than the fanatics of
the desert of the present day. But, wherever
it goes, there are the elements, whether or not
there is the exhibition, of that terrible intolerance of zeal, which, when logically developed,
points the sword at the throat of everyone,
everywhere, who ventures to deny that Mohammed is the great prophet of God.

For this intolerance is an essential element in
Mohammedanism [1] : " there is no precept in the
Koran enjoining love to enemies." The following is said to be a literal translation of a missionary prayer which is offered every evening
in the great university at Cairo :

"O Lord of all creatures, O Allah ! destroy the
infidels and polytheists, Thine enemies, the enemies
of the religion. O Allah ! make their children
orphans and defile their abodes ; cause their feet

[1] *The Mohammedan Missionary Problem*, H. H. Jesup,
30–32.

to slip ; give them and their families, their house-
holds and their women, their children and their
relations by marriage, their brothers and their
friends, their possessions and their race, their
wealth and their lands, as booty to the Moslems.
O Lord of all creatures ! fight Thou against them,
till strife be at an end, and the religion be all of
it God's.　Fight Thou against them until they pay
tribute by right of subjection, and they be reduced
low."

Intolerance ; elemental in all Mohammed-
anism, potential in the Mohammedanism of
Africa, considerably modified as exhibited in
Central Africa ;—this is what we find.

Such is the zeal, such are the methods, such
are the agents—all of which indicate the missionary character of Mohammedanism in Africa.

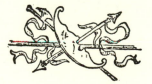

CHAPTER VII

ITS POLITICAL CHARACTER

IN Mohammedanism there is no divorce between Church and State. The modern,
Western idea, that the spheres of religion and
politics are separable, has no place in Mohammedan thought. The teaching and the example
of Mohammed stimulated his followers to rule
as well as to preach, to conquer as well as to
convert. The government of the world is given
to the faithful, so far as they can seize it. The
formula, "Believe, pay tribute, or die," involves
political as well as religious ascendency. The
Sultan is temporally as well as spiritually chief.
The great leaders of Mohammedanism have
evidenced themselves such by warfare as well
as by piety—"half-military, half-religious gen-
iuses, which Islam always seems capable of pro-

ducing." [1] The divine right of kings was never more emphatically asserted, whether by the Stuarts of England or the Bourbons of France, than, for example, by one of the Mahdist generals in a letter to Emin Pasha [2]:

"So now we have come . . . sent to you from his Mightiness the great Chief of all the Muslims, the ever victorious in his religion, who relies on God as the Lord of the world, Khalifa, the Mahdi, may God be gracious unto him! . . . with his sacred orders, which are orders of God and his prophet."

In Africa, as elsewhere, Islam seeks to seize political control quite as eagerly as to make actual converts. Practically, for it, the two are identical. Take for illustration the attempt to proselytise King Mtesa, of the great Uganda kingdom, and to control his successor. This seems to be a principle of Mohammedan advance in Africa— to convert tribes and kingdoms, rather than individuals. In this is revealed the "aggressive spirit" which Dr. Jesup [3] asserts as one of the

[1] R. Bosworth Smith. Quoted in *Christianity, Islam, and the Negro Race*, Blyden, 11.

[2] *Shall Islam Rule Africa?* Rev. L. C. Barnes, 15.

[3] *The Mohammedan Missionary Problem*, H. H. Jesup, 53.

elements of Mohammedanism, and which is evident throughout the whole history of Islam.

But the traditional method of conquest and proselytism combined cannot be applied invariably in Africa. Mohammedanism is not now strong enough in the Dark Continent, or is not zealous enough, to conquer throughout the native kingdoms of the interior as, in the early days of the religion, it conquered throughout Asia and North Africa and in Europe. To some extent a crafty political management of native rulers is attempted. Mr. Arnot[1] describes the efforts of the Arabs " to poison the mind " of King Msidi, of that region, against the English in general and Mr. Arnot in particular. " For the Arabs have been long in communication with the Garenganze country—famous all over Eastern Africa for its copper and salt." King Msidi was wise: after listening to a long harangue from them, he quickly replied: " I am sure I cannot answer your words. I do not know these English people. I certainly do not know this man who is now coming [Arnot];. but one thing I know—I

[1] *Garenganze*, Arnot, 174.

know you Arabs." It is to be borne in mind
that this attempt on the part of the Arabs was,
apparently, rather for trade advantage than for
religious advance ; but throughout all consideration of the Mohammedan problem in Central
Africa, the identification of these two is so close
that the one can hardly be separated from the
other. Particularly is this true concerning the
horrible slave-traffic. The intertwinings of this
infamous business and of Mohammedan proselytism are so close and intricate that suppression has thus far been impossible, and
advance of Mohammedanism and extension of
the slave-trade are almost or quite identical.
The rise of Mahdism in the Soudan gave great
impulse to the slave-trade.[1] It seems to be evident that the Arab in Central Africa is first a
slave-trader, then a Mohammedan. It is necessary to understand this combination of business
and religious interests on the part of the Mohammedan agents, in order to comprehend the advance and influence of Islam in Africa. Of this
attempted political control by Mohammedanism,
another and more striking illustration is to be

[1] *Fire and Sword in the Sudan*, Slatin Pasha, 554.

seen in the restless efforts of the Mohammedans to control the king and kingdom of Uganda— perhaps the most important in Central Africa. It is said[1]

"that when Mr. Stanley's letter from Uganda was published, indicating a willingness on the part of King Mtesa to abandon Islamism and accept Christianity, the Turkish journals took up the subject with great fervour. A Moslem Missionary Society was formed in Constantinople, and subscriptions raised, to send Arab missionaries to confirm King Mtesa in the faith."

The plan may have been dropped, but the fact proves the Mohammedan method in Africa, to control politically. They wanted to gain that kingdom by controlling that king. This has been their course in cases innumerable throughout Central Africa—a crafty interference with native politics, in such way that personal ambition, trade, and religious zeal may be satisfied.

In the African type of Mohammedanism, there is an elasticity that enables it to adapt itself to native ideas. This has been one great reason for Mohammedan political advance. " King Mtesa can retain his one hundred wives

[1] *The Mohammedan Missionary Problem*, H. H. Jesup, 54.

and be a good Moslem still," [1] in spite of the restrictions of the Koran as to such an unnecessary number of helpmates. And it is not simply in matters like this, of royal prerogative and dignity according to native African ideas, that the elasticity of Mohammedanism reveals itself; in the more important concerns of superstitious belief it shrewdly avoids contradiction of native habits and desires, and thus wins political supremacy. " The Mussulman missionaries exhibit a forbearance, a sympathy, and a respect for native customs and prejudices and even for their more harmless beliefs which is no doubt one reason of their success, and which our own missionaries and schoolmasters would do well to imitate." [2]   Such euphemistic statements concerning the " harmless beliefs " of the native African as allowed by Mohammedanism are somewhat surprising when we consider what ideas and practices are included in that remarkable phrase. It is, however, an interesting feature of Mohammedanism in Central Africa, that the native can be largely what he was be-

[1] *The Mohammedan Missionary Problem*, H. H. Jesup, 57.
[2] *Mohammed and Mohammedanism*, R. Bosworth Smith, 58.

fore conversion, and what he still desires to be,
if only he will say, " There is one God and Mohammed is His prophet," and if political ascendency be allowed to the representatives of that
religion.   Control rather than conversion, political power rather than individual change of
heart and life, is what Islam seeks in Africa.

But throughout all this somewhat diplomatic
dealing of Mohammedanism with the pagan
kingdoms of Africa, the main reliance is ever
on the sword, or rather on the spear.   For mili-
tancy has always been an essential feature of
Islam.   A believer must impress the truth upon
the infidel, by force if necessary.   If he dies in
the attempt, so much the better for him—" The
gate to Paradise lies between drawn swords."
The Mohammedan soldier dying in battle, and
the Mohammedan missionary trader dying of
fever, both seeking the conquest of the infidel,
go straight to Paradise.   It is the direct route,
the surest claim.   This thought of death on the
field of battle as a leap into Paradise was the
inspiration of the early conquests.   Doubtless
it has operated largely in fanning the ferocity
of the dervishes of our own day, who have re-

produced in the Soudan the history of the first century of Mohammedanism. Thus the Mahdi spoke, concerning some messengers of his who had been executed [1] :

"My messengers have obtained what they most desired ; when they took the letters from me they sought the death of martyrs, and their wish was fulfilled. The merciful God has granted them their hearts' desire, and now they are in the enjoyment of all the pleasures of Paradise. May God grant that we may follow in their footsteps ! "

In the Turkish Empire now, in all true Mohammedanism, the army is a religious body. It is composed of Mohammedans, and supports Mohammedanism. "A convert to Christianity from Islam [in Turkey] is arrested as a renegade from the conscription. Apostasy from the Mohammedan religion is thus, in Turkey, treason to the Mohammedan state." [2] Even Mr. Bosworth Smith recognises that the sword is "an essential part " of Mohammedanism. [3] The famous ninth sura of the Koran, flashing like the scimitar of Saladin as he whirled it under

[1] *Fire and Sword in the Sudan*, Slatin Pasha, 177.
[2] *The Mohammedan Missionary Problem*, H. H. Jesup, 27.
[3] *Mohammed and Mohammedanism*, R. Bosworth Smith, 169.

the Syrian sun against the Crusaders, has been
the inspiration of the faithful of Africa as well
as elsewhere. For in spite of the quotations
from the Koran which Dr. Blyden adduces to
prove the tolerance of Mohammed towards the
"belief of the book,"[1] and in spite of his attempt to explain the application of the ninth
sura as referring "to the treatment to be ac-
corded by them to those Arabs who join the
worship of idols with that of the true God,"
both the plain meaning of the sura itself and
the development of that meaning in the history
of Mohammedanism prove that war, conquest,
is enjoined upon the faithful against the infidel.
The "Jihad," the holy war, is a conspicuous
feature of Mohammedanism throughout, and
has had its place markedly in the history of
Islam in Africa: in this idea largely lay the
strength of Mahdism.[2]

The native African is by no means the con-
temptible opponent in warfare that the super-
cilious European has sometimes asserted. The

[1] Blyden, *Christianity, Islam, and the Negro Race*, 291.
[2] For some interesting suggestions concerning the "Law of
Jihad," incidentally confirming this statement, see *Faith of
Islam*, Sell, 359.

Waganda army is described [1] as showing a high state of efficiency. The prowess of the Zulus has been attested by Europeans at great cost. The ferocity of the Masais is terrible. The courage and endurance of the Eastern Soudanese won the fear as well as respect of the English soldiers who were repulsed by them. When under the inspiration of Mohammedan zeal, these African soldiers may become absolutely terrible. Sir Garnet Wolseley has said [2]: "I am certain our men would much prefer to fight the best European troops rather than the same number of Mohammedan warriors who were under the influence of Mohammedan fanaticism." What an illustration of this heroic bravery was given by the dervishes in the battle of Omdurman!

Such are the warriors that Mohammedanism sends forth to holy conquest.

"When a heathen tribe or nation is aimed at, a choice is proposed to the chief—the Koran or the sword. On his choosing the Koran, the whole tribe is counted as Mohammedan and the chiefs are pro-

[1] *Uganda and the Egyptian Soudan,* Wilson and Felkin, i., 336.   [2] *Public Opinion,* vii., 210.

moted. But if a refusal is given, war is declared
against the tribe ; the destruction of their country
is the consequence, and horrible bloodshedding.
The aged males and females are massacred, whilst
the salable are led away as prisoners of war
(slaves). As the religion sanctions slave-wars and
slavery, its professors do not sympathise with the
miseries produced by them. They shut their eyes
and tender feelings to these atrocities, and the
gains and profits they reap therefrom are considered their reward as faithful followers of the
prophet " [1]

These Jihads, military expeditions to bring
pagans to the faith, have been " carried on with
wonderful activity and success during the last
fifty years." [2]

The story of Samudu is a startling illustration
of this politico-religious advance of Mohammedanism in Central Africa. He was born about
fifty years ago in the Mandingo country, east
of Liberia. This is a translation of the opening paragraphs of a narrative of his proceedings
by a native chronicler [3] :

" This is an account of the Jihad of the Imam

[1] Bishop Crowther, quoted in *Church at Home and Abroad*,
iii., 594.
[2] Blyden, *Christianity, Islam, and the Negro Race*, 357.
[3] *Ibid.*

Ahmadu Samudu, a Mandingo, an inhabitant of the town of Sanankodu, in the extreme part of the Koniah country. God conferred upon Him his help continually after he began the work of visiting the idolatrous pagans who dwell between the sea and the country of Wasulu, with a view of inviting them to follow the religion of God, which is Islam. Know all ye who read this—that the first effort of the Imam Samudu was at a town named Fulindijah. Following the book and the law, and the tradition, he sent messengers to the king at that town, Sindidu by name, inviting him to submit to his government, abandon the worship of idols, and worship one God, the Exalted, the True, whose service is profitable to his people in this world and in the next ; but they refused to submit. Then he imposed a tribute upon them, as the Koran commands on this subject ; but they persisted in their blindness and defence. The Imam then collected a small force of about five hundred men, brave and valiant, for the Jihad, and he fought against the town, and the Lord helped him against them, and he pursued them with his horses until they submitted. Nor will they return to their idolatry, for now all their children are in schools, being taught the Koran, and a knowledge of religion and civilisation. Alimami Samudu then went to another idolatrous town called Wurukud, surrounded by a strong wall, and skilfully defended," etc.

The career of this West-African illustrator of

Mohammedanism continued unchecked, until he became notorious, not simply in Africa, but throughout. The atrocities of his " holy wars " are indescribable. Thus an official report runs :

" The people of the states to the south of Futa Djallon are pagans, and Samudu makes their religion a pretext for his outrages. He is desirous of converting them to the ' true faith ' and his modes of persuasion are murder and slavery. Miles of road strewn with human bones ; blackened ruins where were peaceful hamlets ; desolation and emptiness where were smiling plantations. What has become of the tens of thousands of peaceful agriculturists, their wives and their innocent children ? gone ! converted after Samudu's manner to the ' true faith.' " [1]

These holy wars, with their horrible confusion of selfishness and religious zeal, have been conducted widely by such tribes as the Fulahs —fiercely Mohammedan. But perhaps the completest illustration is to be found in the history of the Mahdist uprising in Eastern Soudan, with which the name of General Gordon is heroically identified as martyr and General Kitchener as conqueror. It is perhaps the most

[1] Quoted in *Oriental Religions and Christianity*, F. F. Ellinwood, D.D., 205.

conspicuous of all the later eruptions of Mohammedan zeal. A certain Mohammed Ahmed,
born in 1843 in Dongola, claimed to be a true
descendant of Mohammed through his daughter
Fatima. It is said that at the age of twelve
years he knew a large part of the Koran by
heart. He studied under a famous "saint,"
and was ordained as a priest. For fifteen years
he lived an austere life ; fasting, praying, and
meditating on the mission to which he would
eventually give himself. He was aware of the
"shadowy expectations" of the Shiite Mohammedans, who were looking for the speedy
coming of the long-expected Mahdi. He established a school of dervishes ; he obtained
wide repute. There was simply needed a good
opportunity—and lo ! the Mahdi had come. It
was in May, 1881, that he thus proclaimed
himself as from God. The dervishes gathered
around him ; he soon found himself at the head
of an army of fifty thousand men. Bands of
Egyptian forces were sent against him. The
story of the annihilation of Hicks Pasha and
his army of English and Egyptians, about ten
thousand men, is recent history—" not a man

left to carry the fatal tidings to Khartoum."
It was in January, 1885, that the Mahdi captured Khartoum. General Gordon was slain.
The victorious leader of the holy war died of
small-pox soon after; but his lieutenant, the
Khalifa, succeeded him. The English, on the
eve of the battle of August 3, 1889, demanded
of the leader surrender; and he replied, "I
have been sent to conquer the world." The
fanaticism and ferocity of the dervishes were
well illustrated on that field of battle, although
they were completely routed.[1] The fury of
that battle was but a little breath of the fiery
zeal of these later African imitators of the early
conquerors of Islam. The rule and fanaticism
of the Mahdists remained irresistible until this
very year (1898). It is said of a Moslem society, called Sid-es-Senoussi,[2] that its Calif, or
" Divine Lieutenant," had recently under him
" a complete hierarchy of subordinate officers,"
with a probable following of 1,500,000 fierce
fanatics, governed by the same spirit, and com-

---

[1] *The Missionary Review of the World*, iii., 754.
[2] For this sect, see *Church Missionary Intelligencer*, l., 597,
page 6, article by Rev. E. Sell.

mitted to the same end as the Mahdists of the Soudan, all alike aiming at a "speedy, complete, and universal triumph of Islam."[1] A later, probably the last, chapter of this Mahdist history is now being written, in the conquest of the upper Nile province by the English, with a fervour of zeal and fury on the one side, and a perfection of planning on the other, hardly rivalled in history.

Yet again we must observe that throughout such outbreak of apparently religious zeal it is hard to distinguish between what is purely for the advance of Mohammedanism and what is principally for the support of slavery. Concerning the attacks by these very Mahdists upon Abyssinia, from 1885 to 1890, a German missionary expresses his fear that the recent defeat of the Abyssinian army by Mohammedan Mahdists, or dervishes, will result in the "early addition of Christian Abyssinia to the list of countries desolated by the African slave-trade, unless such a result is speedily averted by the proposed conference of the Powers."[2]

[1] *The Missionary Review of the World*, iii., 757.
[2] *Ibid.*, ii., 761.

The whole story of the Arab outbreak in the Lake Nyassa region has as its basis an attempt to preserve the slave-trade, endangered there by the presence of the Europeans. Throughout all this Mohammedan warfare in Africa there seem to be differences of degree, but not of kind. It is all selfishness—principally the slave-trade — and religious enthusiasm combined. In the Egyptian Soudan the religious element predominates. In Lake Nyassa the slave-trade desire is conspicuous. Throughout, the proportions vary, but the elements are the same.

In general, to this political character of Mohammedanism in Africa is largely due the surprising fact that the religion itself has not been absorbed by the paganism of Central Africa. The phenomenon is not to be explained simply by religious zeal. It is the aggressive way in which this zeal has manifested itself, the combination of religion with self-interest, and as well the inspiration of some element of truth, that have sent the followers of the great prophet conquering and to conquer throughout Central Africa. Under this Mohammedan in-

fluence, whether or not due to it, there has
arisen in places a somewhat developed civilisation. Large cities, some public order, military
power, some advance in general condition—all
this is true of the Mohammedan states of the
Soudan. But, on the other hand, there is the
indescribable desolation of large regions immediately south of the Mohammedan kingdoms
of the Soudan, and west of the great lakes—a
desolation so terrible that the heart shrinks
from the consideration of the human misery
involved and the blight upon African humanity.
It may be that Arab influence in Central Africa
must be met, as Lieutenant Wissman has
claimed,[1] only by systematic war measures on
the part of Europe against them. Fight fire
with fire. The political and military ascendency
of Mohammedanism in Africa must be destroyed, if civilisation is to conquer.

[1] *The Missionary Review of the World*, ii., 293.

CHAPTER VIII

ITS MORAL AND RELIGIOUS CHARACTER

IN passing judgment upon a religion, the best
criterion is the effect which it produces
upon the actual life, both in the general morality
which it accomplishes and in the inspiration
from the unseen which it brings. "Conduct is
three-fourths of life." A system of religion
crystallises itself in the external life of its
votaries. It is one of the strange and essential
features of Mohammedanism, not alone in Africa, but throughout, that there is a divorce
between ethics and religion.

"Islam is an intensely formal and ritual system, a
religion of works, not affecting the heart or requir-
ing transformation of life. Fasting, the pilgrimage to Mecca, praying five times a day, testifying
'There is one God, and Mohammed is His prophet,' almsgivings, ablutions, genuflections, circumcision, and repeating the one hundred names

of God, are some of the rites and acts by which the believer purchases Paradise. The minutest change of posture in prayer, the displacement of a single genuflection, would call for much heavier censure than outward profligacy or absolute neglect." [1]

Confining our attention to African Mohammedanism, we have excellent opportunity in North Africa for estimating the moral character and effects of the religion ; for in this region Mohammedanism has had control for a thousand years, with the fullest opportunity for development. Throughout the Soudan and into Equatorial Africa, also, there is much evidence as to the moral character and results of the religion, though of later origin.

Incidentally we may observe that under Mohammedan control the population of North Africa has largely decreased during the millennium now closing.[2] It was Slatin Pasha's observation in Eastern Soudan that "at least seventy-five per cent. of the total population of Eastern Soudan has succumbed to war, famine, and disease, while of the remainder the ma-

[1] *Mohammedan Missionary Problems*, H. H. Jesup, 28, 29.
[2] Speech of Mr. E. H. Glenney, Report of Missionary Conference, London, 1888, i., 29, 30.

jority are little better than slaves."[1]   Throughout his journeys in the desert, Mr. Richardson
reports evidences on every hand of declining
prosperity and decreasing population.   History
reveals a flourishing civilisation in North Africa,
where now is, largely, the abomination of desolation.   But it is a remarkable fact that in
Algeria, where for fifty years the French have
had rule, "the population is increasing pretty
nearly one hundred thousand every year."[2]
From many considerations the inference seems
well founded that Mohammedan control has
been so characterised by injustice, incapacity,
moral degradation, and neglect of the proper
functions of government that life has lan-
guished ; and that, largely, this is chargeable to
Mohammedanism as a religion.   Father Ohr-
walder says of the Soudan that Mahdism
"dragged it back into an almost indescribable
condition of religious and moral decadence."[3]
This will be further, and we think clearly,
evidenced by what we still have to say.

[1] *Fire and Sword in the Sudan*, Slatin Pasha, 623.

[2] Speech of Mr. E. H. Glenney, Report of Missionary Conference, London, 1888, i., 29, 30.

[3] Preface to " *Fire and Sword in the Sudan*, Slatin Pasha.

What Dr. Jesup has said concerning divorce between morality and religion as essential in Mohammedanism in general is proved true concerning Mohammedanism in Africa. Mr. Richardson, from personal observation in the desert tribes, witnessed that " the sum of religion amongst many of the wild tribes is the formula of Mohammed being the prophet of God, fasting, and circumcision"[1]; and Slatin Pasha's summary of Mahdism is even simpler : " The repetition of the five prayers, and the reading of the Kuran, on which no commentaries are permitted to be made, make up the sum total of religion, interspersed now and then with the reading of the Mahdi's instructions and the repetition, twice a day, of the Rateb."[2]   But this formal profession is accompanied by moral degradation, in many respects, throughout these tribes.   Thus there is a sad lack of financial integrity.   "All Tunisian Arabs are robbers."[3]   The Pasha of Tripoli opposed Mr. Richardson's proposed

[1] *Travels in the Great Desert of Sahara*, James Richardson, London, 1848, i., 149.

[2] *Fire and Sword in the Sudan*, Slatin Pasha, 548.

[3] *Travels in the Great Desert of Sahara*, James Richardson, London, 1848, i., 21.

journey into the desert, fearing that it would
interfere with his system of extorting money
from the inhabitants of that country.[1] A large
proportion of government taxes and assess-
ments, throughout this whole region, "gets
into the pockets of the officials."[2] The "Marabout," Mohammedan saint, teacher, and writer
of the village, Mr. Richardson's camel-driver,
was "dishonest when he could be so with
safety."[3] Speaking of these Marabouts, and
alluding to my driver, the Sheik said, "These
fellows pray God and rob man."[4] Slatin Pasha
gives us this picture of Islam, as illustrated by
Mahdism :

"The attempted regeneration of the faith by the
Mahdi, who disregarded the former religious teaching and customs, has resulted in a deterioriation
of morals, which, even at the best of times, were
very lax in the Sudan. Partly from fear of the
Khalifa, and partly for their own personal interests
and advantage, the people have made religion a
mere profession ; and this has now become their
second nature, and has brought with it a condition
of immorality which is almost indescribable. The
majority of the inhabitants, unhappy and discon-

[1] *Travels in the Great Desert of Sahara*, James Richardson,
London, 1848, i., 13.   [2] *Ibid.*, 50.   [3] *Ibid.*, 52.   [4] *Ibid.*, 54.

tented with the existing state of affairs, and fearing that their personal freedom may become even more restricted than it is, seem to have determined to enjoy their life as much as their means will allow, and to lose no time about it. As there is practically no social life or spiritual intercourse, they seem to have resolved to make up for this want by indulging their passion for women to an abnormal extent." [1]

Such hints might be multiplied indefinitely. All know the corruptibility of Mohammedan government throughout. The piracy of the Barbary States in the early part of our present century was encouraged by the Mohammedan government as a means of supplying the public exchequer. [2]

A worse development is to be found in the startling hypocrisy of the religious leaders of Mohammedanism, not simply in North Africa but apparently wherever on the continent the religion goes. Mr. Richardson, early in his journey into the desert, was ushered into the presence of the Mohammedan ruler of a district —an exemplar for that region of Mohammed-

[1] *Fire and Sword in the Sudan*, Slatin Pasha, 560.
[2] *Oriental Religions and Christianity*, F. F. Ellinwood, D.D., 201.

anism pure and undefiled. He said privately
to the Englishman: "Now these people you
are travelling with are barbarians,—you must
humour their whims and respect their religion ;
if they were not now present, we would have
a bottle of wine together." [1] Again, at the interesting city of Ghat, in the very centre of the
Mohammedan desert, the prince said, "Our
Marabouts [religious leaders] are all rogues." [2]
What can be more startling than the picture
which Slatin Pasha presents of the hypocrisy of
the Mahdi, and of his successor, the Khalifa?

"Openly, he showed himself a most strict ob-
server of his own teachings ; but, within their
houses, he, his Khalifas, and their relatives entered
into the wildest excesses, drunkenness, riotous living, and debauchery of every sort, and they satisfied to their fullest extent the vicious passions
which are so prevalent amongst the Sudanese. . . .
The Khalifa, if his health permits it, attends the
five daily prayers most regularly ; and yet, at
heart, no man could be more irreligious. During
all the years in which I have been in the closest

[1] *Travels in the Great Desert of Sahara*, James Richardson, London, 1848, i., 43.
[2] *Ibid.*, 134.

communication with him, I have never once seen or heard him say a prayer in his own house." [1]

Dr. Schweinfurth described the Mohammedan missionaries whom he found at Khartoum as "polluted with every abominable vice which the imagination of man can conceive." [2] Bishop Crowther, the venerable negro ecclesiastic of the Niger region, declares that "the real vocation of the quiet apostles of the Koran is that of fetish peddlers"; and this testimony is confirmed by the explorer Lander. [3] These latter statements may not prove hypocrisy, necessarily, but they clearly indicate the low degree of moral elevation belonging to the Mohammedan missionaries throughout Central Africa. And the Arabs, who are emphatically the representatives and agents of that religion, unblushingly substitute selfishness for self-sacrifice, and slave-hunting for devotion.

It is hardly necessary to specify untruthfulness as one of the moral characteristics of Mo-

---

[1] *Fire and Sword in the Sudan*, Slatin Pasha, 375, 547.

[2] Quoted in *Oriental Religions and Christianity*, F. F. Ellinwood, D.D., 211.

[3] *Ibid.*, 211.

hammedanism throughout. This vice is a
prevalent one throughout the East, and among
non-Mohammedan peoples; but the fact that
Mohammedanism has not corrected it, and does
not in general produce truthfulness, is an indication of the character of the religion. "Are
you so foolish, Yakob, as to believe everything
a Mohammedan tells you?" was the question
which they asked Mr. Richardson in the
desert.[1]

Hints of something like order, morality, and
self-control are found here and there. "There
is no crime worth naming in the oases."[2]
"Ghat is a country of peace."[3] "The Touariks
never steal."[4] One of the characteristic features of Mohammedanism is the self-control demanded through the feast of Ramadan. This
fast for thirty days is said to be conscien-
tiously observed by all the faithful—even in
Africa; involving abstinence from food and
drink throughout the daytime.

[1] *Travels in the Great Desert of Sahara*, James Richardson, London, 1848, i., 427.
[2] *Ibid.*, ii., 36.
[3] *Ibid.*, 74.
[4] *Ibid.*, 149.

" If there were a railway from West Africa to
the Red Sea and you wished to avail yourself of it
in a journey to Egypt during the fast month, (you
might perhaps accomplish the journey in seven
days,) you would during those seven days pass
through a route where you would find every man,
woman, and child in good health observing the
fast. On the entire route, four thousand miles,
you would notice that the fires were out in the daytime. No other part of the globe presents such a
sight—sixty million people fasting at the same
time." [1]

This statement by Dr. Blyden seems to
us somewhat exaggerated. Investigation will
make it evident that it would be an exceedingly difficult task so to plan a railroad in
Central Africa that it shall lead through four
thousand miles of a Mohammedanism so strict
as here specified. But there is sufficient truth
in the assertion to indicate a degree of moral
restraint, beneficial or otherwise, as exerted by
the religion and characterising it.

In general it must be said that throughout
Mohammedan North Africa "the most terrible
unrighteousness, the grossest degradation, cou-

[1] *The Church at Home and Abroad*, vii., 412.

pled with the vilest immorality" exist.[1] The reference is to the Mohammedan states north of the desert. This is confirmed by the testimony[2] of one who lived eighteen years in Morocco—"one of the most intensely Mohammedan countries in the world." He says, "There does not exist a more degraded and corrupt country on the face of the earth." It is hard, or impossible, to find an eulogist of the moral condition created by Mohammedan control in North Africa through the last one thousand years.

We have already referred to the fact that throughout the desert, largely by force of circumstances, a better moral condition prevails. It is not Mohammedanism that has produced this superiority, but human isolation and need. The stern life of the desert necessitates some confidence and faithfulness man with man; and it gives chance for all possible inspiration from what of the great common stock of truth is presented in Mohammedanism. But it is not

---

[1] Speech of Mr. E. H. Glenney, *Report of Missionary Conference*, London, 1888, i., 29.

[2] New York *Tribune*, April 7, 1893.

Islam as a system that is to be credited with this moral betterment. The desert has always been man's walking ground with God.

Passing now to Mohammedan civilisation south of the desert, we have Mr. Stanley's testimony concerning the general condition of affairs in the Egyptian Soudan. In the revulsion following the complete overthrow of General Gordon's control, there was an awful lapse; "Venality, oppression, and demoralisation replaced justice and equity and righteousness." But this was largely a return to the old order that had become established under Mohammedan dominancy. In Kordofan, a Mohammedan state in Eastern Soudan, "the moral character of the people is about as bad as it can well be."[1] In Darfur, lying immediately east of Kordofan, the morals of the people are very lax.[2] Throughout that part of Western Soudan of which Bishop Crowther had knowledge there is, as he testifies,[3] "full licence of all sinful enjoyments." The awful licen-

[1] *Uganda and the Egyptian Soudan*, Messrs. Wilson and Felkin, ii., 310.
[2] *Ibid.*, ii., 276.
[3] *Life of Samuel Crowther*, 103.

tiousness of Mahdism in the Eastern Soudan is written on almost every page of Slatin Pasha's wonderful tale, *Fire and Sword in the Sudan*. The testimony is well-nigh, or quite, unanimous, that the moral character of Mohammedanism throughout the Soudan, as throughout North Africa, perhaps excepting the desert, is unspeakably bad. The attempts to compare it, favourably, with some bad features of European and American civilisation, do not parry the charge—for the evil excrescences of the latter are not to be compared with the essential character of the former.

As the matter upon which we are now dwelling is all-important for a correct understanding of Mohammedanism in Africa, it is necessary to specify two or three points that have been thus far only suggested in general : intemperance, sensuality in the strict use of that term, and slavery. These three classes of evil indicate clearly the moral status of Islam in Africa.

Dr. Blyden claims that " throughout Central Africa there has been established a vast ' Total Abstinence Society.' "[1]   He asserts that such

[1] Blyden, *Christianity, Islam, and the Negro Race*, 201.

is the influence of this society, that "where there are Moslem inhabitants, even in pagan towns, it is a very rare thing to see a person intoxicated." But Mr. Richardson, even throughout the desert regions of enforced abstinence and self-control, testifies concerning the Moslems that "many of them do not fail to intoxicate themselves with everything . . . which comes in their way."[1] As to the demoralisation of the natives by rum, many non-Moslem tribes "were not more given to the use of intoxicating liquors than were the Moslems about Musardu and even among those like the Kabyles of North Africa."[2] In Tunis "alcohol is the chief foe of the missionary's work." "Mohammedan insobriety is notorious." Hear the confession of the Sheik Hassan.[3]

"Once, travelling with Gordon," he remarked, "I fell ill, and Gordon came to see me in my tent. In the course of our conversation I told him that I was addicted to alcoholic drinks, and that I put

[1] *Travels in the Great Desert of Sahara*, James Richardson, London, 1848, i., 315.

[2] Dr. Gracey in *The Missionary Review of the World*, i., 382.

[3] *Fire and Sword in the Sudan*, Slatin Pasha, 35.

down my present indisposition to being obliged to do without them for the last few days. This was really my indirect way of asking Gordon to give me something; but I was mightily disappointed, and, instead, received a very severe rebuke. 'You, a Moslem,' said he, 'and forbidden by your religion to drink wines and spirits! I am indeed surprised. You should give up this habit altogether; everyone should follow the precepts of his religion.' I replied, 'Having been accustomed to them all my life, if I now gave them up my health must suffer; but I will try and be more moderate in future.'"

Further, we have the somewhat significant fact that Turkey, the banner-bearer of Islam, voted at the Berlin Conference for free rum in the Congo Free State.[1] We cannot avoid the conclusion that Dr. Blyden romances somewhat concerning his great total abstinence society of Central Africa. Mohammedanism, asserting temperance if not total abstinence, fails to enforce its command in Africa—as, we are told, elsewhere. The Arabs themselves are the chief importers of intoxicating spirits into Africa.[2]

In attempting to illustrate the moral character

[1] *The Church at Home and Abroad*, iv., 27.
[2] *The Missionary Review of the World*, i., 99.

of Mohammedanism in Africa by reference to sensuality, we approach a matter upon which it is unpleasant to write. It must be borne in mind that Mohammedanism in its very constitution makes a distinct appeal to the ruling passion of human nature. It allows, to the faithful, four wives and limitless concubinage. Mohammed, by special dispensation, granted unto himself fifteen or more wives—and proclaimed a message from heaven rebuking himself for undue continence. The marvellous growth of Mohammedanism throughout the world has been ascribed by some to the sensual indulgence which this religion authorises. But that cannot wholly account for such a majestic triumph over mankind; "It is a calumny on men to say that they are aroused to heroic action by sugar-plums in this world or the next. In the meanest mortal there lies something nobler." [1] It must be borne in mind that while the religion of Mohammed allows licence in certain respects, it teaches such restrictions in other respects that licence is to some degree counterbalanced by restraint. But the restraint

[1] *Heroes*, Thomas Carlyle, 64.

is on matters comparatively unimportant ; and the licence is in certain lines along which evil nature runs almost irresistibly. Because the fast of Ramadan is insisted upon for thirty days a year Mohammedanism is not to be excused in the practically unlimited sensuality which it allows. Islam is essentially sensual.

Concerning the Moors of the towns of North Africa it has been said, " No people are more sensual and impure." [1] And Mr. Glenney in his address at a conference said [2]: " I dare not in a company like this tell you of the condition of these countries, morally—or rather immorally. I could not tell you of the vile practices that are done in these lands."   Slatin Pasha in investigating the country between the Blue and White Niles, found a trade-centre in which was " an immense collection of young women, the property of the wealthiest and most respected merchants, who had procured them and sold them for immoral purposes, at high prices. This was evidently a most lucrative trade." [3]

[1] *Travels in the Great Desert of Sahara*, James Richardson, London, 1848, i., 174.

[2] *Report of Missionary Conference*, London, 1888, i., 29.

[3] *Fire and Sword in the Sudan*, Slatin Pasha, 5.

Perhaps no more significant hint could be given than that presented by Mr. Richardson [1] when he said, " The Mohammedans claim that a saint or Marabout cannot have too many women or wives, which they say assist their devotion—a sentiment which they pretend to have received from Mohammed himself by tradition." Apparently this utter lack of sensual control characterises the whole of Mohammedan civilisation in Africa. We find the rotten fruitage of a religious system that contrives, essentially, the destruction of the family relation throughout, and the consequent degradation of women. [2]

The third feature of the moral character of Mohammedanism in Africa upon which we would dwell is seen in connection with the slave-trade. There is opened before us the whole question as to the connection of Mohammedanism with slavery. A dark story, absolutely unwritable and incredible to Western civilisation, presents itself to us. We cannot enter upon it at length. It lies in direct

[1] *Travels in the Great Desert of Sahara*, James Richardson, London, 1848, i., 57.

[2] *The Mohammedan Missionary Problem*, H. H. Jesup, 34–37.

connection with what has just been said concerning Mohommedan sensuality. " One of
the greatest obstacles to the suppression of
the slave-trade was the facility which it afforded
Moorish and Arab merchants to indulge in
sensual amours.[1] Sir William Muir attributes
to this the persistence of the Mohammedans in
the slave-trade. He claims that,[2] "so long
as a free sanction to this great evil stands
recorded on the pages of the Koran, Mohammedans will never of their own accord cease to
prosecute the slave trade."

In the African slave-trade we have what
Livingstone called " the open sore of the
world." Not only is Mohammedanism the
religion of the slave-driver; Mohammedanism
sanctions the slave-trade, and is responsible, in
the last analysis, for the wide-spread demand
that has prolonged the export slave-trade of
late. We recognise the fact that Mohammedanism restricts the slave-trade somewhat—
so far as Mohammedans are concerned. While

[1] *Travels in the Great Desert of Sahara*, James Richardson,
London, 1848, ii., 348.
[2] *Oriental Religions and Christianity*, F. F. Ellinwood,
D.D., 192.

there are Mohammedans that are slaves, and while the common assertion that Mohammedans are exempted from slavery is an error,[1] it is certainly true that throughout Africa the Mohammedan slave-traders make their raids rather upon tribes that are not Mohammedans. But "to attack slavery in Mohammedan countries is to interfere with institutions to which Islam gives a religious sanction."[2]

It is not necessary here to enter into a description of the awful inhumanity and evil of the Mohammedan slave-trade. A shaded map[3] indicates that the region of slave-hunting extends from about five degrees north of the equator to twenty-five degrees south of it ; indeed, almost throughout the continent, excepting a narrow district along both eastern and western coasts. Also, that "slave caravans have been embarked as late as 1889" along both eastern and western coasts of this whole stretch, throughout the districts that are supposed to be under the control of the great

---

[1] *The Arab and the African*, S. T. Pruen, 210.

[2] *The Church Missionary Atlas*, i., 33.

[3] *The Arab and the African*, S. T. Pruen, 226.

Powers of Europe. A slight apology, or at least an attempt at fair statement, is made by a missionary, Dr. Pruen[1]; he says that most of the slaves are purchased by the Arabs from the native chiefs of the interior, and that "these slaves are stated to be either the scum of the native villages of whom the chiefs are glad to be rid, or else the prisoners taken by the up-country chiefs in their frequent fights." Also,

"a smaller trade is done by fraud. Small parties of natives or single individuals are enticed into a caravan to sell food, and are then seized ; or else in time of scarcity the people of a half-starved village are encouraged to join themselves to a caravan on the assurance that there is plenty of food a few miles ahead. But after the few miles' march the plenty does not make its appearance, and the unfortunate people sadly recognise the fact that they have said farewell to their freedom."

Also, parents sell their children for food to passing caravans. Dr. Pruen evidently makes the most favourable statement possible—out of a spirit of fairness. He asserts that

"the Arab does not as a rule ill-treat his slaves. When an unfortunate slave is seized with illness,

---

[1] *The Arab and the African*, S. T. Pruen, 212, 250.

and unable to continue the journey, he is, as a rule, if the caravan is near the hunting ground, killed by the Arab in charge. If this custom were not the rule, the whole caravan would get ill at the next station. If it is necessary to transfer the body of slaves from the interior to the coast, then the only way is to kill those too ill to travel."

But these statements give faint idea of the shocking barbarities that are really committed, and of the cataclysmic desolation that is wrought by the slavers. Surrounding a village, the Arabs set fire to the huts; as the frightened people emerge, the men are killed and the women and children are seized. The indescribable savagery at the moment of the attack is but a hint of the long-drawn horrors of the march. All possible devilishness in human nature is exhibited throughout. A practical extermination of tribal life, at least a destruction of the prosperity and primitive civilisation of vast and populous regions, is accomplished.

" The Arab wreaks a ruin even greater than the annihilation of tribes outright ; he keeps the region in a perpetual ferment, sets chief against chief to prevent combination, and either makes tools of the tribes likely to become dominant, or shatters

them by instigating rebellion among their de-
pendents."[1]

Dr. Livingstone bore witness to the vast desolation accomplished in a short time in the
regions through which he travelled.[2] So also
does Mr. Stanley ; and so do all the later travellers throughout Equatorial Africa. Cardinal
Lavigerie estimated that two million lives are
massacred in obtaining the four hundred thousand slaves annually brought to the coast[3];
but this statement seems to be considerably
within actual facts.[4] The social disturbance
throughout the vast continent, arising from
these slave-raids, can readily be imagined.
"Whenever Livingstone crossed the slave-path
he found the natives suspicious and inclined to
be unfriendly."[5] "Until the advent of the
slave-dealer, the native tribes lived generally
at peace among themselves, but since then a
great change has taken place."[6]

Slavery is an indigenous institution in Africa.

[1] *The Missionary Review of the World*, iv., 428.
[2] *Life of Livingstone*, Montefiore, 101, 116, 153–156.
[3] *Ibid.*, 155.
[4] *The Missionary Review of the World*, iv., 428.
[5] *Life of Livingstone*, Montefiore, 51.
[6] *Uganda and the Egyptian Soudan*, Wilson and Felkin, 209.

The Arabs did not introduce it ; but it is they who have made the export trade in slaves from Central Africa, and who have developed the unutterable horrors of the business. Because Islam expressly sanctions slavery and does not operate to check its abominations, though Mohammedans have power to do so, the religion of Mohammed must be held largely responsible for what has been here merely suggested. The moral character of Mohammedanism in Africa, the inevitable result of that religious system which some have attempted to extol, is written in letters of blood and fire in the history of the African slave-trade throughout the last fifty years of this century. The question concerning the forced stoppage of this horrible traffic is indeed a difficult one. England has entered heartily into the work, as also have some other European nations. But the lust and greed of the traders, the difficulty of access into the slave-raided regions, the power of the Turkish Pashas and army and wealthy classes,[1] the ready market for slaves throughout the Mohammedan lands

[1] *Uganda and the Egyptian Soudan*, Wilson and Felkin, ii., 217.

of North Africa and Asia, above all the sanction of Islam, make success most difficult.   The
shrewdness of the Arab traders in avoiding obstacles is almost phenomenal.   And the question is further complicated by the assertion
that with increasing difficulties in the way of
selling prisoners of war as slaves to the Arab
traders, intertribal warfare in Central Africa
becomes more fatal if not more cruel.   All attempts thus far to abolish the trade have been
but feebly effective.   The true solution lies in
easy access for foreign influence by railway, or
at least by good roadway, from north to south
and from east to west throughout the continent,
and in the development of a legitimate commerce among the natives.   But the power of
the Mohammedan Arab in Central Africa must
first and completely be broken.   The introduction of foreign influence throughout the Dark
Continent will gradually accomplish this.

But little is to be said concerning the higher
characteristics of Mohammedanism as a religion.
Islam in Africa is of the earth, earthy.   In
passing from the realm of mere morality into
that of higher religious conception, we make a

transition that is not at all a familiar one to the
African Mohammedan. He makes but little of
what thought of God and of the future life and
of final accountability his religion brings to him.
Doubtless, to the Mohammedan of the seventh
century higher truths were real and vivid;
but his successors of the nineteenth century
in Africa are degenerate. It is indeed sad
to see the utter lack of spiritual elevation
throughout the sixty millions, more or less, of
Mohammedans in Africa. Here and there is
observable an outburst of the old enthusiasm,
in which the thought of God and the outlook
into the spirit life are real and dynamic. In a
vague way, even now, the essential doctrines of
Mohammedanism, the person of God, Divine
providence, the anticipation of Paradise, are
supposed to be held in mind. The very existence of the mosque, supposed to be zealously
established wherever Mohammedanism goes,
even if only an ordinary bamboo and thatched
hut dignified by that exalted name, serves to
prevent the native from forgetting entirely that
there is one God, and that his communication
with that God in prayer is not only a possibility

but a duty. It is probable that there are places in Central Africa where Islam as a religion, dealing with things beyond this life, is still a reality.[1] Such revivals as that of the Wahahbees and of the Mahdists serve to show that Mohammedanism at times and in places can make real the unseen. But, in general, these higher thoughts and this inspiration from above have but little part in an African Mohammedan's life. Dr. Pruen quotes Palgrave as accurate in his characterisation of the Arab as evincing a settled resolution to prefer the certain to the uncertain, the present to the future. If true of the Arab, far more of the Mohammedanised pagan.

" Shall I abandon the pleasures of the pure wine-
        goblet
    For all they tell me about milk and honey here-
        after ?
    Life, and death, and resurrection to follow,
    Stuff and nonsense, my dear Madam."[2]

Such are the lines of a popular Arab poet—and they indicate sadly the utter earthliness, even sensuality, of Islam as a religion in Africa.

[1] Blyden, *Christianity, Islam, and the Negro Race*, 378.
[2] *The Arab and the African*, S. T. Pruen, 259.

CHAPTER IX

THE CHANGE FROM PAGANISM

WE have already seen that Mohammedanism has obtained complete control
in Africa throughout the north and the desert;
is practically supreme throughout the line of
kingdoms immediately south of the desert ;
is predominant throughout the Soudan. Also,
that there are many Mohammedan settlements throughout Equatorial Africa, small
and sparse; and that Arab traders reach far
south, even to the line of Mozambique. There
are said to be about sixty millions of Mohammedans now in Africa.[1] What change has been
effected by the conquering religion?

The early overthrow of Christianity in the
north of Africa was complete, so far as the

[1] *Encyclopedia of Missions*, ii., 121.

destruction of Christian institutions is concerned. By division, sectarian strife, bitterness
of so-called Christian spirit, neglect of true
spirituality, the Church of Christ in those regions had left its first love. The warning had
been unheeded: "Remember therefore from
whence thou art fallen, and repent, and do the
first works; or else I will come unto thee
quickly, and will remove thy candlestick out of
his place, except thou repent."[1] Mohammedanism, fleet as an Arab steed, keen and cruel
as a scimitar's edge, overwhelmed an unworthy
and unspiritual Christianity—and so completely
that absolutely nothing was left. The change
at that time in that region was complete as
possible; and it may have been, for a while at
least, improvement. We are not prepared to say
that the enthusiasm of the early Mohammedan
conquerors was not higher and better than the
corrupt Christianity which they overcame. But
in its far-reaching results, through the ten centuries that have intervened, the inherent evil
of Mohammedanism has manifested itself in
that region. No possible corruption of Christ-

[1] Rev. ii., 5.

ianity could have brought such a blight upon a fair portion of the earth's surface as Islam has accomplished in North Africa.

There are many evidences that Mohammedanism did not so completely penetrate the desert tribes of Africa as in Arabia and the surrounding Mohammedan regions. At the time of the first conquest of the desert it may be that Mohammedanism was somewhat modified by the paganism which it supplanted; but practically this religion has so developed itself under desert influences that we have now in the Sahara, perhaps, the purest and most typical Mohammedanism. Down to the Soudan Islam has had free course—though hardly to its glorification. Whatever may have been the paganism of that region, a complete change was wrought long ago.

But the question as to the change from paganism becomes more interesting, and more difficult, as we approach the races south of the desert—the more recent conquests of Islam in Africa. Much has been claimed that proves on investigation to be startling exaggeration.

The Mohammedan states of Northern Soudan doubtless contrast favourably in their civilisation with the savagery of some Central-African tribes. But the question arises as to whether this is real change from paganism, due to Mohammedan influence? or is it due to a natural superiority in the natives involved? The Hausas, the Fulahs, the Mandingoes, are splendid races of men; their native civilisation would be far higher than that of many African tribes. It may be that to some extent credit is due to Islam for abolishing " cannibalism, human sacrifices, the burying of living infants, the horrors of fetishism, belief in witchcraft, intemperance," —as Mr. Bosworth Smith claims [1]; though, so far as our present investigation has been able to reach, this is largely unsubstantiated assertion by Mr. Smith. It may possibly be provable to some extent concerning the narrow line of Mohammedan states of which we have spoken. On the other hand, there is an overwhelming mass of testimony to the effect that in general the change from paganism effected by Mohammedanism is so small as to be practically nothing. Even in the hotbed of Mahdism the

[1] *The Church at Home and Abroad*, iii., 595.

Bedeyat are merely nominal Moslems. "If
their chiefs are asked by Mohammedans to re-
peat the creed, they can say, 'There is no God
but God, and Mohammed is His prophet.' But
beyond this they know nothing; they are utterly ignorant of the precepts of the Kuran,
and never pray as Moslems." [1] "The negro
tribes that have been won to allegiance by the
prophet of Mecca are Moslem in little more
than name." [2] "The Bournous, Fulahs, Mandingoes, and Jaloofs, who profess Islam, have
done little more than abandon some of the
rites of paganism." [3] We have the authority
of Bishop Crowther, whose testimony our continued study into these matters inclines us to
take without question, to the effect that "even
in those districts where Mohammedanism has
got the firmest hold, it has not superseded but
rather grafted itself upon the superstitious
demon-worship of the natives everywhere." [4]
The explorer Lander asserts, "Those who
profess Mohammedan faith among the negroes

[1] *Fire and Sword in the Sudan*, Slatin Pasha, 114.
[2] *Encyclopedia of Missions*, i., 9.
[3] *The Missionary Review of the World*, i., 382.
[4] *Life of Samuel Crowther.* Preface, ix.

are as ignorant and superstitious as their idolatrous brethren; nor does it appear that their having adopted a new creed has either improved their manners or bettered their condition in life."[1]

Take for illustration the kingdom of Uganda under Mtesa, and the conversion of king and kingdom to Mohammedanism. Uganda "is by far the most powerfully organised and (in its way) civilised state which has been found in Central Africa."[2] King Mtesa was a young man in 1861. A little later he came under the influence of Arab traders, and became by profession a Mohammedan; but apparently his conversion consisted largely in a change of costume—simply putting on Arab clothing. Mohammedanism took but little hold on the mass of his people; though the course of King Mtesa was followed in a nominal way by his chiefs.[3] Later, Christian missionaries were received into his court; Mtesa himself now became an accepter of Christianity, about the

[1] *Oriental Religions and Christianity*, F. F. Ellinwood, D.D., 211.

[2] *Church Missionary Atlas*, 58.

[3] *The Story of Uganda*, S. G. Stock, 34.

year 1877. But in 1879 Mtesa and his chiefs
publicly prohibited both Christianity and Mohammedanism, and returned to their heathen
superstitions.[1] Again a change of sentiment
—it could hardly be called conviction—in 1881.
Such religious agility on the part of King
Mtesa enables us to see clearly that Mohammedanism, as Christianity, was for him little
more than a name, and that while nominally
converted to Islam, at least for a while, his
people remained practically unaffected. The
story of this native African kingdom would
have been lost for us were it not for the close
connection of these changes with recent exploration throughout that region.   But it leads us
to question the reality of Mohammedan conquest, and the degree of Mohammedan influence, in other kingdoms, the story of whose
conversion we do not chance to know so
clearly. All reliable testimony leads irresistibly to the conclusion that Islam in Central
Africa has accomplished little more than a
superficial change—and largely not even that.
Dr. Pruen writes, " I have never seen a Swa-

[1] *The Story of Uganda*, S. G. Stock, 77.

hili [Mohammedan] perform any other religious duty than to turn a sheep or goat towards
Mecca before he cut its throat." [1]   Again : " I
do not know any single instance in Eastern
Equatorial Africa of a pure native who has
become a true and earnest Mohammedan.
There are many nominal ones.   The nominal
Mohammedan cares practically nothing for religious rites, and never performs them when alone,
nor when in company unless in the presence of
an Arab." [2]   This indifference of the nominal
Mohammedans of Eastern Equatorial Africa
to the demands of their religion seems to be
largely a characteristic throughout.   The Khalifa himself never prayed in private. [3]   There
are earnest and true Mohammedans, but they
are largely of Arab or half-Arab parentage.
So far as the original tribes are concerned,
Mohammedanism is merely a thin veneer,
where it exists at all.   Its semi-civilisation is
due as much to the superior capacity of the
natives whom it has reached as to any inherent

---

[1] *The Arab and the African*, S. T. Pruen, 264.
[2] *Ibid.*, 297.
[3] *Fire and Sword in the Sudan*, Slatin Pasha, 547.

elevating power of Islam itself. The doctrine
of one God is doubtless a great leap upward
from paganism ; but it will be found that even
this central and essential thought is hardly
grasped by the Central-African Mohammedan.
Instead, a modified fetichism is all that the
followers of the great prophet have been able
to effect.

This is a somewhat startling assertion, when
we remember that the doctrine of the unity of
God is the great and essential cry of Islam from
east to west. It is its boast and glory that
idols are shattered by it wherever it goes ; that
the clouds of polytheism are dissipated by it
as the mist by the sun. But, strangely, what
Mohammed did in Mecca when he broke the
idols, what his zealous followers did in such
lands as India where they met with a developed polytheism, Mohammedanism has been
incapable of accomplishing in Central Africa.
The native form of religion eludes the attack—
for the simple reason that it presents no idols
to break.

To understand this failure of Mohammedanism to produce marked religious change in

Central Africa, it is necessary to look briefly at
the native religion—if it may be called such.
Throughout the larger part of the Dark Continent a terribly superstitious and debasing form
of fetichism prevails: it is one of the lowest
manifestations of the natural religious instinct
of man.   There is throughout, apparently, a belief in a Supreme Power of God—but so vague
as to be utterly indefinable.   The thoughts, or
rather fears, of the natives are centred in the
race of demons which mixes with human life.
An oppressive fear possesses all.   These demons are largely, or entirely, evil agents.   A
universal faith in witchcraft arises, with all its
terrors.   The ordeal by fire and water is applied on slightest cause or occasion.   A superstitious faith in charms arises naturally.   There
has not been sufficient advance, either intellectually or socially, to develop the more definite
conceptions of polytheism.   Hence Mohammedanism is brought face to face simply with
a vague imagination and a terrible fear.   It
lifts the mallet to break the image—and strikes
nothing but air.   The fetiches that play so
large a part as objects of African reverence are

not idols, gods, or representations of gods;
they are simply objects in which supernatural
power is supposed to reside.

Thus it will be seen that Mohammedanism
finds it easy to assert its doctrine of the *one
true God.* The idea of Mohammed as the
Great Prophet, also, is easily acceptable by the
natives. The real point at issue between Mohammedanism and African fetichism is in the
superstitious fear of the native, manifesting
itself in charms and in the abominations connected with witchcraft. Now the peculiarity
of Islam in Central Africa lies in the fact that
it has absorbed and assimilated this superstitious fear. It may be that it substitutes its own
fetiches for the original native objects of superstition ; but it does not essentially change that
superstition. "As the ruder tribes [in the
Mandingo] region do not addict themselves to
the intellectual habits of the Mandingoes, it
has been found necessary to adjust that faith
to the necessities of the case ; and to temper
some of the mummeries of the fetiches with
the teachings of Islam."[1] The Koran is made

[1] *Journey to Musardu*, 39.

little more than a fetich. Charms, largely passages from the Koran written on slips of paper
and enclosed in cases, or bound around beef-
bones, worn on the person or buried in the earth,
are most efficacious in peace or in war, in any
extremity.[1]   Again we quote Bishop Crowther's
assertion—" the real vocation of the (so-called)
quiet apostles of the Koran, is that of fetish
peddlers." And Mr. Lander says of these
Mohammedan teachers, " These Mollahs pro-
cure an easy subsistence by making fetiches—
writing charms on bits of wood which are
washed off carefully in a basin of water and
drunk with avidity by the multitude."[2]   Mr.
Felkin found this fetich-like superstition in the
Egyptian Soudan; he writes, "Some of the
Mohammedan priests profess to write charms
which render their possessors perfectly bullet-
proof."[3]   It extends even into the purer Mohammedanism of the desert; for Mohammed,

[1] *Journey to Musardu*, 33; Blyden, *Christianity, Islam,
and the Negro Race*, 203.
[2] *Oriental Religions and Christianity*, F. F. Ellinwood,
D.D., 211.
[3] *Uganda and the Egyptian Soudan*, Wilson and Felkin, ii.,
59.

the Islamic Marabout who undertook the guid-
ance of Mr. Richardson's camel in his desert
journey, applied verses of the Koran to the
eyes of his wife's sister, "which were more
efficacious than all my physic." Some of these
bits of paper with the name of God written on
them were steeped in water and swallowed by
the patient. This superstition of swallowing
bits of paper with the name of God and verses
of the Koran written on them, as well as the
water in which the paper is steeped, is prevalent as an infallible remedy in all Mohammedan
Africa.[1] Islam in Central Africa, and to some
degree in Northern Africa, is little more than
a slightly modified fetichism.

That but slight change from paganism is
wrought by Mohammedanism in Africa is
evident in other matters as well. The act of
prayer, so conspicuous and important in typical
Mohammedan regions, becomes increasingly
neglected as one penetrates southward into the
continent of Africa. Mr. Wilson observed that
during the whole time in which some Uganda

---

[1] *Travels in the Great Desert of Sahara*, James Richardson,
London, 1848, i., 58.

Mohammedans were with him—save on one
occasion when his boat was in extreme danger
—he never knew them to pray, though they
professed to be strict Moslems.[1] Throughout
the whole range of literature concerning Central Africa, so far as we have been able to
observe, so little reference is made to the Mohammedan act of prayer—so conspicuous in
Arabian and Turkish Mohammedanism—that
we are forced to the conclusion that it is practically lost in Central Africa. Also, Mohammedanism has practically left pagan polygamy
intact, " in principle and in practice." [2]

So far as religious manifestation is concerned,
the change from paganism wrought by Mohammedanism in Central Africa is but slight. Yet
civilisation of a certain sort has certainly advanced into Central Africa with Mohammedanism. Islam is a step, even if only one step, in
advance of paganism. The cry " There is no
God but God and Mohammed is His apostle "
—" an eternal truth and an eternal lie "—at

[1] *Uganda and the Egyptian Soudan*, Wilson and Felkin, i.,
119.
[2] *The Missionary Review of the World*, i., 382.

least contains a more advanced assertion of the great truth than anything that paganism presents. Behind that cry, and uttering it, is a more or less zealous band of warriors and teachers, to enforce the acceptance of this short and simple creed. They bring with them ideas of another, a higher, civilisation. The modifications of pure Mohammedanism which African paganism accomplishes are not sufficient entirely to cut off this connection with an outer and higher world. As an indication that Islam, in its advance through Africa, has accomplished some improvements of social condition, even though but little modification of religious thought, take the fact that the Arab has been the means of introducing the Swahili language throughout Central Africa—thus making a medium of general communication, not simply for the Arab trader, but for the Christian missionary.[1] The language of the slave-trader has been utilised as the language of the Word of God.

In the matter of education is the clearest indication of what Islam has accomplished in

[1] *The Church at Home and Abroad*, xii., 462.

African paganism. Undoubtedly there is, in
the religion of the great prophet, some incentive to learning of a certain kind. Reverence
for the Koran incites to study of its language.
But, in general, the inspiration leads no farther
than into the sacred book and its accompanying
traditions. There is but little idea of general
education. The devotee learns the Koran by
heart and copies the characters—though " it is
believed by many persons that the Arabic
learning of our Mandingoes, in reading and
writing from the Koran, is merely mechanical,
or a mere matter of memory." [1] But, without
question, the earnest Mohammedan is prompted
strongly to learn Arabic that he may read the
Koran for himself ; he acquires thereby a
means of receiving new ideas which, to some
extent, are uplifting. Teachers of Arabic go
through the country. Schools are established.
Dr. Blyden [2] gives a glowing picture of the way
in which African youth rush into Mohammedan
Arabic literature and culture. He says [3]:

[1] *Journey to Musardu*, 40.
[2] Blyden, *Christianity, Islam, and the Negro Race*, 205-211.
[3] *Ibid.*, 360,

"Throughout Mohammedan Africa, education is compulsory.   A man might now travel across the continent, sleeping in a village every night except in the Sahara; and in every village he will find a school." But we do not find such statements verified; on the contrary there is much to render them doubtful. The most that we can assert is that Mohammedanism provides an incentive to a certain amount of intellectual culture, and that considerable intellectual activity accompanies it, where the proper development of its influence is allowed. The mere fact that Mohammedanism inculcates a pilgrimage to Mecca at least once during the lifetime, and that for various reasons Mohammedans in Africa are great travellers,[1] will serve to indicate and explain much of this educational stimulus.

Mohammedanism has done something towards developing agriculture in some parts of Africa, and business enterprise throughout, save as the slave-trade has wrought desolation rather than prosperity. But there is in Africa, particularly in the north, trade " untainted by

[1] Blyden, *Christianity, Islam, and the Negro Race*, 215.

slavery." [1]   Interchange of sympathy between the Mohammedan communities undoubtedly stimulates interchange of goods.

In one great point, Mohammedanism makes marked change. It certainly develops self-respect in the native, so far as its essential ideas really possess him. "The negro who accepts Mohammedanism acquires at once a sense of the dignity of human nature." [2]   The true Mohammedan believer knows God, believes himself to be favoured by God, is taught to assert himself as an equal among believers—even if a slave. Theoretically, and to some extent in fact, Islam makes a man of the pagan. Costume is an indication ; King Mtesa signalised his acceptance of Mohammedanism by putting on the Arab costume.

Comparatively little elevation of religious ideas, a single step in advance in general civilisation, some educational stimulus, some development of self-respect,—all this we recognise as accomplished by Mohammedanism in Africa.

[1] *Travels in the Great Desert of Sahara*, James Richardson, London, 1848, preface, xxv.

[2] Mr. R. Bosworth Smith—quoted in *Christianity, Islam, and the Negro Race*, Blyden, 11.

Yet it is not possible for us to go to the extreme
to which such writers as Bosworth Smith, Canon
Taylor, and Winwood Reade go—when they
assert, for example, that Mohammedanism " is
better adapted to the country than Christianity "[1]; that the progress of any large part
of the negro race is in proportion to its Mohammedanism[2]; or that " Mohammed redeemed
the Eastern World and his followers are re-
deeming Africa."[3] We cannot fully agree
even with Dr. H. P. Smith as he says, " We
cannot doubt that even now it [Islam] carries
into the heart of Africa a civilisation and a
morality that are an immense advance," etc.[4]
For a correct understanding of the problem it
is most important to see clearly that unwar-
ranted exaggeration of statement has been
made so frequently and publicly as largely to
mislead. A careful investigation will surely
show that the imagination of some men has
unaccountably run riot in dealing with Islam
in Africa.

[1] *The Church at Home and Abroad*, iii., 68.
[2] *Mohammed and Mohammedanism*, R. Bosworth Smith, 56.
[3] *Encyclopedia of Missions*, i., 9.
[4] *The Bible and Islam*, Dr. H. P. Smith, 318.

In this connection it must be noted that there is a tendency towards fixedness, a stereotyping process, that characterises Mohammedanism everywhere. As it fastens itself upon an inferior community it tends to raise that people up to its level—but to fix them there. It cuts off the possibility of further advance, save so far as its essential influences may be counteracted from without. This is startlingly illustrated in North Africa: the Barbary States were stereotyped centuries ago. This tendency is essential in the system. The Mohammedan believes that the Koran is the last and unalterable revelation from God—it holds the Mohammedan world fast; and it is only too evident that it has not within itself any supernatural adaptation to human needs and advance. Also, in the repressive effects of that fatalism which, though perhaps not a doctrine, is yet the practical result of Mohammedan teaching, we have additional reason for this tendency of Mohammedanism to stop immovably at a certain point.

"Nothing in the world is so energetic as a Mohammedan nation in its youth and nothing is so

truly feeble as a Mohammedan nation in old age.
. . . A Mohammedan nation accepts a certain
amount of truth, receives a certain amount of civilisation, practices a certain amount of toleration.
But all these are so many obstacles to the acceptance of truth, civilisation, and toleration in their
perfect shape. The Moslem has just enough on
which to rest and pride himself and no longer feels
his own deficiencies." [1]

Mr. Sell says of the great Mohammedan religious order of the Sanúsiyah : [2]

"The great object of the founder 'was to erect
an impassable barrier to the progress of Western
civilisation and the influence of Christian powers
in Muslim lands.' In these ardent propagators of
a great Pan-Islamic movement it is possible that
Great Britain and France will find deadly foes
harder to conquer than the Khalifa and his dervishes."

In estimating the change wrought in African
paganism by Mohammedanism, while recognis-
ing some advance, we must consider this draw-
back,—that essentially it lifts the natives a little
way, only to fasten them at that point the more
obstinately. We have seen that the point of
elevation is indeed low.

[1] *History and Conquest of the Saracens*, E. A. Freeman, 57.
[2] *Church Missionary Intelligencer*, January, 1899.

We may well question as to whether Islam
has been, on the whole, of advantage to Africa.
The enthusiastic claims of those who have held
it as the highest possibility for Africa, and
even of those who have claimed it as the best
preparation for the introduction of Christianity,
must be largely discounted.   When we remember the responsibilities of Mohammedanism for
the slave-trade, when we consider the vast
desolation and cruelty wrought under the
sanction of Mohammed, when we remember
that such evils as polygamy and divorce and
slavery "must continue to flow so long as the
Koran is the standard of the people "[1], when
we consider that an almost insuperable barrier
is raised by Mohammedanism against anything
higher and better, we may well feel inclined to
assert with a recent writer[2] that " Islam is at
the bottom of the weight of ills under which
Africa is suffering."   Is real advance wrought
in African paganism by Islam ?   Little or none.
Indeed, so superficial, from this point of view,

[1] Sir William Muir—quoted in the *Missionary Atlas*, i.,
70.
[2] Quoted in the *Encyclopedia of Missions*, i., 9.

is the Mohammedanism of large parts of Africa that "the conversion of a whole pagan community to Islam need not imply more effort, more sincerity, or more vital change than the conversion of a single individual to Christianity."[1]

[1] R. Bosworth Smith—quoted in *Oriental Religions and Christianity*, F. F. Ellinwood, D.D., 220.

CHAPTER X

THE AFRICAN TYPE OF MOHAMMEDANISM

ISLAM is Islam the world over. But there are distinctions and differences important to notice. In Africa there is a markedly distinct type of Mohammedanism. In the development of this religion in the Dark Continent, under the peculiar conditions involved, there has been a somewhat startling divergence from the old type. The natural development of Islam in other countries has produced a something in many respects different from the ideal of the great prophet and of his immediate successors; yet we behold in Turkey, Arabia, and Egypt what may be called the orthodox type—in contrast with what is to be found largely in Central Africa, and in varying degrees throughout North Africa. At least to our imagination, old Islam presented almost the ideal of heroism,

of zeal, of a faith true even if incomplete. Orthodox Islam in these evil days presents a de-
terioration into weakness, sensuality, sterility
—youthful Islam grown old and decrepit and
bad. In African Islam we have a renewal of
youth — characterised by an enlargement, a
superficiality, a selfish and materialistic greed, a
combination of all that has been proved bad,
with but little of what has been proved good,
both in the youth and the age of Islam.

" All the bad, salient features of Mohammedanism
are asserted—intolerance, polygamy, slavery, un-
natural crime, contempt of human life, an over-
weening pride—while the better things to be found
in the Koran, and the learning and the refinement
of the polished Mohammedan of India, and Persia,
and Turkey, are totally absent." [1]

Let us notice some particulars. See in the
first place that African Mohammedanism is
characterised by aggressiveness. This was the
marked characteristic of Mohammedanism as it
sprang from the brain of the great prophet,
and was asserted by his immediate successors.
It was with a mighty aggressiveness that they

[1] *The Missionary Review of the World*, iii., 204.

began, and continued, their wonderful career
of conquest. Aggressiveness was inherent in
the system. In its decrepitude, Mohammedanism has now largely ceased the attempt to
assert itself by force against the infidel nations
around ; indeed there is a great question as to
whether or not Mohammedanism in general
has of late really made any advance outside of
Africa.

But in the Dark Continent Islam has, throughout this century, been markedly aggressive—
making large advance. There are many indications which lead one to believe that its progress, even in Africa, has now ceased ; and
that, perforce, its aggressiveness there, too, is
curbed. With the entrance of European influence into Africa, Arab and Mohammedan establishment must cease advance ; rather, must
recede. But it is in Africa that later Mohammedanism has shown itself on a large scale as
nearest the original type in its aggressive en-
ergy. That mighty impulse, crystallised in the
Koran, which forces the believer to swing his
sword over his infidel neighbour, demanding
confession or life, has manifested itself for a

while irrepressibly in the Mohammedan tribes of Africa. And it is in the region of Eastern Soudan that we have seen the mightiest revival of the old Islamic spirit—in the furious aggressiveness of the dervishes, sweeping the soldiery of England and Egypt from the field, annihilating armies, seeking to obtain a country in the name of God and for His prophet the Mahdi. The conquests in Central and Western Soudan indicate this same aggressiveness.

It is said that throughout a large part of Mohammedanism in the world there are indications of a general unrest. It may be that the extraordinary activity of Islam, lately, in Africa, is but a part of a general stir; but the fact remains that here we have this restlessness turned into aggressive progress, exhibited to a degree nowhere else shown throughout the Mohammedan world. It distinguishes the African type.

Again, we notice that African Mohammedanism is characterised by superficiality. Early Islam, in its progress, left behind it only true believers, or slaves of believers, or the dead bodies of the unconvertible infidel. Its work was thorough—as is that of the forest fire. This same completeness of conversion, or extinction, characterises the orthodox Mohammedanism of to-day, in so far as it has power. But a marked feature of Mohammedanism in Africa lies in this,—that it burns only in patches, and merely the underbrush. Mohammedan states border upon pagan tribes; Mohammedan individuals are surrounded by unbelievers; Mohammedan aggressiveness seeks to reach them—but not to exterminate them; Mohammedan conquest is only on the surface of individual or social life—as we have seen. The African Mohammedan is still a pagan.

To some extent this superficiality of religion —in marked contrast to the old Islamic intensity of religious zeal and to modern Turkish intolerance—is to be seen even in North Africa. It is more clearly shown in the elasticity with which Islam adapts itself to the habits of Central African life and thought. It is also indicated in the fact that African Mohammedanism, markedly, pays less attention to tradition than to the text of the Koran [1]; as with the Phari-

[1] *The Church at Home and Abroad*, vii., 411.

sees of old Judea, intense devotion to Mohammedanism should be marked by the careful ob-
servance of tradition, and neglect therein proves
a lapse from the old orthodoxy. In many ways
it can be shown that African Mohammedanism
is superficial, as compared with the penetration
of Islam into the heart and life of its early
adherents, and even of its later orthodox
professors.

This leads us to a third suggestion. African
Mohammedanism is characterised by a lessened
zeal in proselytism. A fiery fury led the early
Mohammedans into a career of proselytism
that seemed limited only by the reach of the
race of man ; they would win souls for God
and His prophet, even if in so doing they must
die and enter Paradise. Perhaps nowhere
throughout human history, at least on so large
a scale, can we find a similar exhibition of zeal
in proselytism. But the Arab charger has
been tamed into a draught-horse; much of his
spirit is gone. And yet in the Mohammedanism of Turkey, and perhaps India, there is still
a longing for the conversion of the infidel ; and
we hear of more or less attempt at propaganda

in America as elsewhere. The zeal for proselytism is not dead, even in Africa. But it is
surprising to find with what tolerance the
average African Mohammedan will view the
infidel or pagan ; and how comparatively easy
is access to him on the part of the Christian
missionary. In those days when the believer
could not look with the least degree of allowance upon dissent from his doctrine, it would
be hardly possible to imagine such tolerance
as is exhibited in many places by the African
Mohammedan of to-day. Were the old zeal
burning within him, he would seek to make
converts by the old and orthodox methods ;
but that is not the characteristic of the African
Mohammedan in general. With many and
great exceptions, this lessening zeal in proselytism may be said to distinguish the present
type of Islam in Africa. The fiery zeal of
Omar, the fury of Khaled "the sword of God,"
have worn themselves out—or have been transferred to Paradise.

Again, African Mohammedanism is now
characterised by a decided materialism. The
things of this life are considered rather than

the things of the spirit life. It is the material, rather than the spiritual, that occupies thought and fills ambition. This is in clear contrast to the old Mohammedanism—which dwelt largely on the thought of God and imagination concerning Paradise. So real was the unseen to the Mohammedan warrior of the older days that he entered battle, rushed upon death, with the joy of a bridegroom. So clear was his assurance of the favour of the Divine Being that he went forth in a strength almost supernatural. Throughout human history it has always been this realisation of the unseen that has most completely armed and inspired the children of men.

But we cannot help seeing, particularly in the Mohammedanism of Central Africa but as well to some degree throughout the Mohammedanism of the whole continent, that the unseen has largely lost its power. We have already referred to the fact that the higher, the immaterial, elements of religion seem to find but comparatively little place in African Mohammedanism. Prayer is neglected, the mosque is inconspicuous, the Koran is largely a charm to protect from earthly evil, Paradise is far off and vague. The African Mohammedan is occupied too largely with thoughts as to what he shall eat and drink, if not as to the wherewithal he shall be clothed.

It may be that this characteristic, materialism in his religion, is due partly to the qualities of the negro mind and the circumstances of negro life. We would repeatedly urge the truth that the negro, though not inferior to the white man, is different. We gladly recognise possibilities in the character and constitution of the negro which will render him in some respects superior to his paler brethren, counterbalancing inferiority in other respects. Yet it must be acknowledged that, partly because of his racial tendencies and his environment, it seems impossible for him to emphasise the immaterial features of Mohammedanism, as they have become the mighty inspiration of the believer in other places and times. The fact remains that the negro Mohammedan is decidedly earthly in his religion.

This evident neglect of the spiritual, in view of the material, is also due largely to Moham-

medan methods of advance—particularly in
Central Africa.   When a tribe is placed in the
unpleasant dilemma of choosing conversion or
slavery, and as, naturally, it prefers nominal conversion and Mohammedan dominancy to the
horrors of a slave-raid, the religion thus selfishly established can have but little chance to
develop in its converts those spiritualities towards which it is supposed to lead, though
ruthlessly.   The negro proselyte has obtained
relief and security for himself ; he goes his way
and is content.   The demands of his religion
are not such as to open the skyward vision of
his soul.

But no amount of explanation concerning
this characteristic of African Mohammedanism
in general will do away with the fact that it is
an evidence of real decline.   His religion is
largely in material satisfaction, and for earthly
gain.   Even in North Africa and the desert
there are many indications of such materialism ;
and, in spite of the furious religious revivals of
the Mahdis of both Eastern and Western Soudan, the average Mohammedanism of the continent is too largely limited by an earthly horizon.

Notice another characteristic: African Mohammedanism is cruelly selfish.   It can hardly
be claimed that Islam, at any time or in any
place, has been unduly gentle or considerate.
A selfish cruelty was breathed forth by the
prophet himself, and has characterised the
religion throughout.   But in Africa its development in this respect has been awful.   Particularly is this revealed in the slave-trade, which,
in some parts of Africa, has become almost
identical with Mohammedanism.   " Slavery, as
the Arabs themselves declared, was their very
life." [1]   In those regions wherein the Arab is
the Mohammedan representative and missionary the cruelties of the slave-trade are, verily,
a part of his religion ; and as African Mohammedanism sanctions and succours the African
slave-trade, this selfish cruelty becomes a general characteristic.   " Slavery is a very essential
part of their system, civil, social, and religious." [2]
And the startling fact is that this cruelty of
slavery is, apparently, in contradiction to the

[1] *The Missionary Review of the World*, v., 717.
[2] Dr. Hamlin in *The Missionary Review of the World*, i.,
864.

teaching of Mohammed, at least as proclaimed
by the Turkish Minister at a conference held
at Brussels a few years ago. This representative of Mohammedanism, on hearing an address
by Cardinal Lavigerie on the " African Slave-
Trade," took occasion to protest, saying that
the teaching of Mohammed is contained in the
words, " the worst of men is he who sells men."
The Cardinal replied :

" I do not know in Africa a single Mohammedan
state, great or small, the sovereign of which does
not permit, and more often himself practises upon
his subjects, and in ways the most barbarous in
atrocity, the hunting and sale of slaves throughout
all Africa ; it is only Mohammedans who organise
and conduct the bands who ravage it by slave-raids
and by the sale of slaves. . . . I do not know
. . . a single Mohammedan who does not ad-
vocate slavery on principle. Never to my knowledge has any teacher . . . of the Koran . . .
protested against this infamous traffic. On the
contrary, in their conversation they recognise it all
as authorised by the Koran for true believers as
regards infidels." [1]

And the demands of Turkish harems for
mutilated male attendants, under the implied

[1] *The Church at Home and Abroad*, v., 109.

if not explicit sanction of their religion, are such as involve cruelty beyond expression. It is estimated that in Africa thousands of boys are killed every year in accomplishing this purpose. " But it is a good and pious as well as a profitable work and pleasing to Allah and the prophet." The subject presents a fearful amount of sanctified cruelty; it is an essential part of Islam.[1] Enough has been said to indicate a revolting characteristic of African Mohammedanism. Its cruel selfishness stands out conspicuously. In this it differs, not essentially but in degree, from the modern Mohammedanism of some other countries.

One further characteristic must be observed : modern African Mohammedanism is not impregnable to the attack of civilisation or of Christianity. Even in Morocco, the religious centre and hotbed of Islam in Africa, Christianity has effected entrance. Mr. E. F. Baldwin reported in the year 1889[2] concerning a successful work in Mogador, Morocco ; there was severe persecution, but " accessions have been constant, and

---

[1] *The Missionary Review of the World*, i. 865.
[2] *Ibid.*, ii., 525.

everyone baptised has renounced Mohammedanism." He reported great opposition ; but
the mere fact of his presence in Morocco is
significant. " It seems strange, as it is, that in
Mohammedan Morocco the Moslems are free
to change their religion." [1] We may be inclined to doubt the full accuracy of this statement; but that it has been made indicates
something. Later information suggests a revival of Mohammedan intolerance in Morocco. [2]
But we have the fact that in North Africa, even
in the most violently Mohammedan region, access to Islam has been had, and attack has been
made, which, under like circumstances, could
hardly have become possible in some other
Mohammedan countries.

Whether or not we shall be sustained in our
assertion that North-African Mohammedanism
is more accessible to the " infidel " than the
intolerant orthodoxy of the past and even of
to-day,—though there are many indications of
this,—it will be readily acknowledged that in
those large regions of Central Africa wherein

[1] *The Missionary Review of the World*, iv., 604.
[2] *Ibid.*, v., 608.

Islam has nominal supremacy, the "infidel" trader and missionary have easy entrance so far as intolerance against non-Mohammedan religious belief is concerned. Islam in Central Africa seems to be far removed from the old ideal. The Christian missionary may find difficulty in approach; but it is largely caused by pagan fear, and not by Mohammedan prejudice. A tribe that is only nominally Mohammedan will, of course, feel but little of that intense hostility to another faith which, for example, is constantly shown by Islam against Christians in the towns of Asia Minor. As a result, the Mohammedanism of Africa is not to be judged as we estimate the Mohammedanism of Asia. It is not a solid mass, intolerant, prejudiced, resistant, impregnable. He who estimates the possibilities for European influence and Christian conquest in Mohammedan Africa by the criteria used in judging of Mohammedan Turkey will be led far astray. African Mohammedanism is not thus impregnable to attack.

Such are certain characteristics conspicuous in African Mohammedanism. It will be seen that we have here a distinct development of the religion of the prophet and of the Koran. It is made clear that we have in Africa a form of Islam in some respects nearest to the primitive type, but in other respects far behind the Mohammedanism of other lands. " It will be another thousand years before Islam can bring the African to the cultured and lettered prejudices of Moslem civilisation, such as bind its subjects at Cairo, Ispahan, Delhi." [1]   But in view of the presentation that has been made, particularly in this chapter but throughout as well, we cannot refrain from an expression of astonishment that it should ever have been seriously imagined, as apparently by Canon Taylor and others, that Mohammedanism can be a sufficient step upward for the African pagan and a sufficient substitute for Christian civilisation. Such assertion partakes too largely of the thought of a Mohammedan shoemaker in Morocco, who spoke as follows to an English traveller, a Christian missionary, who was clothed in Moorish costume:

" You must not wear our clothes, as they are given to us by God to set forth the character of our re-

[1] *The Missionary Review of the World*, i., 501.

ligion ; and He gave you Europeans your clothes
to set forth the character of your religion. You
see these garments of ours, how wide and flowing
they are ; our sleeves are loose, and we have easy
fitting slippers. As our clothes are wide, so is our
religion,—we can steal, tell lies, deceive each other,
commit adultery, and do all manner of iniquity
just as we wish ; and at the last day our prophet
Mohammed will make it all right for us. But you
poor Europeans ! you have tight-fitting trousers,
tight-fitting waistcoats, and tight-fitting jackets.
Your clothes are just like your religion—narrow.
If you steal, cheat, deceive, or tell lies, you stand
in constant fear of the condemnation of God." [1]

[1] *The Church at Home and Abroad*, xii., 544.

CHAPTER XI

THE GREAT SOLUTION

A VAST problem has been opened before the world—the civilisation of a continent. We mean by that, the establishment of such conditions of life, the erection of such social institutions, that mankind in Africa may have opportunity for " life, liberty, and the pursuit of happiness "; that the African may have a better chance to develop his possibilities for time and eternity. The responsibility falls upon those who are now engaged in making the map of Africa. European and Western civilisation must take this matter in hand ; the duty cannot be evaded. The far future of African humanity is being determined in this present. What that future shall be, what it should be, the means of attaining the ideal, all constitute a great problem. To accomplish the solution will demand not only the wisest thought of statesmen but the sublimest self-sacrifice of Christians.   Let us look at some solutions suggested for the great problem of African redemption.

Some hold up Mohammedanism—as an end in itself, or, better, as preparatory to Christianity.   The mighty hold which Islam now has upon Africa, the great advance that it has lately made, all projected into future and imagined enlargement, have seemed to some to be clear indication of a providential purpose to establish this religion as supreme in Africa. Theoretically, its acceptance throughout would be a great advance upon paganism ; though we have seen that practically it has thus far accomplished but little, and that it simply blocks the way to real advance.

It is said that many enlightened Africans are inclined to think that Islam is, at least for the present, the great factor in the solution of the question.[1]   Mr. Bosworth Smith lays himself open to the charge of believing that Moham-

[1] Blyden, *Christianity, Islam, and the Negro Race*, preface, xiii.

medanism is destined to control the larger part
of Africa and to become, in and through itself,
the great solution :

'That Mohammedanism may, when mutual misun-
derstandings are removed, be elevated, chastened,
uplifted by Christian influences and Christian
spirit . . . I do not doubt ; and I can therefore look forward, if with something of anxiety,
with still more of hope, to what seems the destiny of
Africa . . . that the main part of the continent,
if it cannot become Christian, will become what is
next best to it—Mohammedan." [1]

It may be that Mr. Smith modifies his expres-
sions, perhaps opinions, by later statements.
But he has suggested an idea that is certainly
held by some, and positively asserted.

A more plausible, if not probable, presentation
of Mohammedanism as a factor in the great
solution is made by those who assert that
Islam is simply preparatory to Christianity.
Some development of Christian civilisation is
recognised as the end to be striven for—social
institutions such as characterise Christianity

---

[1] Quoted in *Christianity, Islam, and the Negro Race*,
Blyden, 25.

and are pervaded with its spirit. But such thinkers claim that Mohammedanism is a real and necessary step towards the ideal. They think that African paganism cannot, or will not, receive Christianity directly. They assert that the dilution of truth and elasticity of religious demand presented in Mohammedanism will serve as a ladder up which the African may climb into the heights of fuller truth and social possibility. Through Mohammedanism and its civilisation, to Christianity and its civilisation, is their cry. It is said that General Gordon cherished the idea " of utilising the Moslem power, with Khartoum as a centre, for carrying on the work of civilising the millions of Equatorial Africa." [1] He seemed to think that Mohammedanism possessed enough truth for this regenerating work. This seems to be included in the basal ideas of the proposed Gordon Memorial University in the Soudan. And much that Dr. Blyden says leads one to think that he, himself a negro and a remarkably intelligent thinker upon the great problem of African civilisation,—though we have been

[1] Blyden, *Christianity, Islam, and the Negro Race*, 379.

obliged to dissent from many of his assertions,—
is inclined to consider Mohammedanism as an
efficient factor in accomplishing the final and
full redemption of the continent.

Our opinion on this matter has been made
evident. We believe that Mohammedanism
in Africa is definitely opposed to civilisation.
While it contains truths that are indeed higher
than the vague terrors of paganism, it also contains such errors and evils as must neutralise
all the real good that might be accomplished
by its supremacy. These evils are essential in
the system ; as they develop themselves in the
lines directed by African human nature they
produce results that are disastrous. No approach towards anything like Christian civilisation has thus far, in general, been made by
Mohammedanism in Africa—nor can it be
made. The so-called Mohammedan kingdoms
and civilisation of Northern Soudan prove
themselves hindrances, not helps, in progress
towards the ideal for which we would strive.
Islam sanctions such social evils as polygamy,
easy divorce, and slavery ; it annihilates with
the sword all freedom of thought and private

judgment in religion ; it shuts out, so far as it can, all possibility of improvement; it can never be otherwise than a hindrance to real civilisation.

It has been wisely observed that in the conflict between civilisation and barbarism, Islam must be the loser.[1]   The great tides of human tendency, like the tides of the ocean, beat against arbitrary human obstruction, only to overcome in the end. " The Sultan and his officers are constantly obliged to obtain new legal decisions, legalising what is religiously illegal and contrary to the convictions and belief of the readers of the Koran."[2]   In Africa, as in the Turkish Empire, Mohammedanism will find itself unadaptable to necessary changes, and yet unable to resist.   Already indications of this are to be seen in Central Africa.   Since the advent of European power and the pressure of European civilisation and ideas, the Arab power is decidedly checked, and apparently on the decrease.[3]   We think it evident that Mo-

---

[1] *The Mohammedan Missionary Problem*, H. H. Jesup, 94.
[2] *Ibid.*, 95.
[3] *Public Opinion*, vii. 330.

hammedanism in Africa, while up to late date
making rapid advance, is now checked in its
progress.   Apparently it has, at least throughout a large region, degenerated into a slave-
raiding organisation.   With the opening of the
continent, this feature of Islam will be largely
restricted, at least so far as concerns the horrors
of traffic in the exportation of slaves ; though
so long as Islam is what it is, and so long as it
has any control whatsoever, the institution of
domestic slavery will hardly be uprooted.   But
the check to Mohammedan advance in Africa,
now evident, is but the sign of a final dissolution,
for the system cannot accommodate itself to
modern civilisation.   This opinion concerning
the retrogression of Mohammedanism in Africa
is confirmed in many ways.[1]   Indeed, one writer
goes so far as to assert that " the political down-
fall of the system [Mohammedanism throughout the world] is thus an accomplished fact."[2]
The ground of his assertion is that Mohammedanism is nothing without political power ;

---

[1] *The Church at Home and Abroad*, ii., 486.

[2] Dr. Schreiber, of Barmen, quoted in *The Church at Home
and Abroad*, xi., 523.

and that the lands wherein it has held sway
are rapidly becoming subject to Christian nations.   This, and more, is emphatically true of
Islam in Africa at present.   It cannot survive;
it is a hindrance and not a help to the higher
civilisation.   Mohammedanism is not to be
considered a factor in the great solution.

It has been thought that in Liberia we have
the key that shall eventually open the lock.
The negro colonisation of Africa seemed to
promise great things.   It was indeed a holy
enthusiasm that led the founders of the Colonisation Society to project their scheme.   It
may be that they were largely influenced by
the thought that this plan would solve great
questions for America as well as for Africa, in
finally settling the burning issues of slavery
in the Western Republic.   But their scheme involved a definite attempt to solve the problem
of the redemption of Africa.   They believed
that by sending Christian negroes from America and the West India Islands to Africa, there
would be made possible an establishment of
Christian civilisation there that should in the
end permeate the continent.   A little nation

has been started on the western coast of the
great continent, and, in pursuance of this plan,
it has been recognised by the great Powers.
Autonomy has been granted to it, and vast
possibilities opened for it. It is said that it
has been growing steadily, if not rapidly ; that,
including the tribes under its control, its population is already a million in number, governed
largely by Africans from America. It may be
that there are large possibilities in that country ; but we cannot help thinking that the early
anticipations of the Liberian colonists can
never be realised. The black population of the
United States and of the West India Islands
prefer to remain where, originally, the cruelty
of man placed them.

Liberia has made but little impress upon the
continent—and for long can accomplish but little. It may be that in the far future it will
stand as a type for a great African nation—
Africa governed by Africans; though in the
partition of Africa among the great Powers, it is
more than probable that this nation will seek
a protectorate, and perhaps absorption. Germany has already proposed this, but to Eng-

land or America Liberia looks with preference.[1]
But the central thought of the plan—foreign
negroes imported into Africa, to rule and civilise—does not contain the promise and potency
of success. Liberia and negro colonisation
cannot be considered as a factor in the great
solution.

The civilisation of Africa must be accomplished by Christianity and commerce—hand in
hand. The conjunction of these two may seem
strange; really, it is close and vital. Nowhere
is their mutual interdependence more clearly
seen than in the consideration of the problem
concerning the redemption of the Dark Continent.

"Conquest by railroads" is a phrase that
means much in these days. But it means more
for Africa than for any other part of our globe.
The railroad in Africa is the preliminary solution of our problem—for over it alone can pass
that commerce and that Christianity which
shall accomplish the civilisation of the continent. The two great material questions concerning Africa are how to create wants, and

[1] See *The Independent*, l., 579.

how to open channels of trade. Until the natives want articles manufactured elsewhere, they
will not be impelled to develop what their
own country can produce; until safe and easy
pathways for trade can be opened, such desire
for interchange, even if it should exist, cannot
be gratified. And until commerce opens the
way, Christianity, and consequent civilisation,
will make but little progress. Livingstone's
idea was correct—open Africa for commerce,
then Christianity will go in. He planned his
life with far-seeing sagacity, and he devoted
himself to the preliminary work of exploring
the continent, in order to find possibilities for
European entrance into the vast unknown.

But to make possible this great solution, it
is absolutely necessary that European influence, or control, should predominate throughout the continent. The answer to the problem,
at least so far as the immediate future is concerned, lies largely in the sway of such nations
as England and Germany throughout the Dark
Continent. The Conference held at Brussels,
September 12, 1876, is for Africa what the Hejira is for the Mohammedan,—that point from

which all succeeding history must date. Directly resulting from that meeting was the Berlin Conference of 1884, which gave birth to the
Congo Free State; and throughout these years
gradually and greedily the great Powers have
been clutching coast-line and interior, appro-
priating vast regions in absolute control, or
establishing "spheres of influence" wherein
they may be predominant, until now of the
11,864,600 square miles of Africa but a small
part remains unappropriated. This mighty
appropriation of territory has been severely
criticised, in some respects justly; perhaps the
partition should have been with more regard
to native and natural rights. But adverse
critics are too apt to forget that the whole
problem of African civilisation, with its world-
wide complications, rests absolutely on the establishment of such European influence. This
control may be most selfishly and unjustly exerted; for illustration, see the absolute selfishness of the Portuguese claim to control over
Nyassaland,—abetting the slave-trade therein,
—threatening war against England but a few
years ago. Negotiations are said to be opened,

or closed, by which Portugal's possessions in
South-eastern Africa will be transferred to England ; but the matter is, as yet, kept secret.
Portuguese control in Africa has been largely
to effect an extension of the rum-traffic and a
maintenance of the slave-trade.[1]   And the German efforts at African colonial control have not
been in all respects ideal. Also, some bad
effects of European influence in Africa stand
out markedly ; particularly in connection with
the introduction of rum and firearms. Some
years ago it was said that from eighty thousand
to one hundred thousand rifles, mainly the
disused arms of European standing armies,
were imported annually into Zanzibar alone,[2]
largely to arm the Arabs that they might
desolate the interior ; and it is said that intoxicating liquors to the value of over five millions of dollars were recorded in one week, at
the island of Madeira, as bound for Africa—
incredible as it may seem.[3]

Much may rightly be said against the way

---

[1] *The Church at Home and Abroad*, vii., 206.
[2] *The Missionary Review of the World*, iii., 862.
[3] *Public Opinion*, xiii., 361.

in which European influence has thus far been exercised in Africa. Entrance has been made for the bad perhaps more largely than for the good. But the door has been opened. It is possible now to civilise Africa. Something has already been accomplished in that line. Commerce has already succeeded in checking slavery on the Congo.[1]   And in this year (1898) the new Congo railway has been opened from Matadi to Stanley Pool. The " Cape to Cairo " railway has been accomplished as far as Bulewayo towards the north and Khartoum towards the south ; the two thousand miles intervening will be covered in some way before long. Mr. Stanley testifies[2] that the Arabs have been crushed within the sphere of influence in East Africa, and that the suppression of the slave-trade therein is assured, if not accomplished. " The partition of Africa among the European Powers . . . was the first effective blow dealt to the slave-trade in inner Africa. The final blow has been given by the act of the Brussels Anti-

[1] *The Missionary Review of the World*, iii., 43.
[2] *Slavery and the Slave-Trade in Africa*, H. M. Stanley, 63–75.

Slavery Conference." Troubles have recently arisen for Germany from an unskilful exercise of colonial power. The British East African Company has been hampered in its most important operations in connection with Uganda and the Egyptian Soudan. But in general much has been already accomplished, and the pathway has been opened to future and fuller achievement. When more railroads are built, as they surely will be, there will come rapid growth from the seed-sowing already accomplished. It is said that plans are now being prepared to utilise the Nile cataracts for the production of electric power on a scale larger even than at Niagara Falls, for the illumination and stimulation of the Dark Continent. Africa is assured for civilisation, and civilisation for Africa.

But something more than commerce is needed, as we have seen, to accomplish what is desired. All civilisation, everywhere, exists, and is of avail, only as connected with religion. It is only through a linking of the human with the divine, of the seen with the unseen, that man can secure that self-development and enjoyment which are the objects of what we call civilisation. The influence of trade alone can never sufficiently curb the passions and develop the possibilities of what is now African savagery. The twin factor in the great solution is religion.

Mohammedanism has been tried, and, as we have seen, is found wanting. Christianity, the world-need, is emphatically the need of the Dark Continent. As compared with Islam, Christianity offers to Africa faith instead of mere submission.[1] And Christianity offers God as present in humanity in the person of Jesus Christ, instead of God as a stern dispenser of fate, who from His far-off habitation has merely sent a prophet to speak His word. Christianity presents a code of morals difficult of attainment, but rendering possible the development of purity in individual and social life; while Islam forces and fastens the shackles of immorality upon its followers. There is an inspiration to infinite possibilities in Christianity, there is an indwelling life, pushing onward divinely; in Islam is the rigour and fixedness of death. Compare the life of Jesus with that

[1] *Shall Islam Rule Africa?* Rev. L. C. Barnes, 24.

of Mohammed, and therein we shall find a true
comparison between Christianity and Mohammedanism as applied to the problem of the
civilisation of Africa. We readily recognise
that Christianity has as yet made but little
entrance, comparatively, into Africa. But the
fact that Islam has made such large entrance,
and has accomplished so little, and can accomplish nothing more, leads us the more confidently to assert that the religious element in
the great solution can be found in Christianity
alone. To accomplish this, Christianity must
antagonise and supplant Mohammedanism in
Africa. Conflict, not comity, is what must en-
sue. Those who claim Mohammedanism as an
assistant in the civilisation of Africa, and an-
ticipate an harmonious co-operation between
Islam and Christianity in the development of
the African races, are living in a land of dreams.
The hardest part of the struggle for the full
conquest of the African continent by the powers
of life and liberty will be found in this need of
overthrowing Mohammedanism. The struggle
against paganism is easy in comparison with
that against Islam.

Yet the inevitable conflict of Christianity with Islam in Africa is not so desperate as some may think. The unconquerable tenacity with which Islam has sustained itself in the Turkish Empire has been in imagination transferred to Africa; thus making, by inference, the contest almost a hopeless one. But we have endeavoured to show that the peculiar type of Mohammedanism which we find in Africa presents a great modification in this respect. Islam in Africa will be comparatively easy for Christianity to overcome. Its superficiality, its comparative languor, its emphasis of doctrines held in common by Christian and Mohammedan,[1] render the work of the Christian missionary more easy and hopeful than elsewhere in Mohammedan lands. The influence of the Christian nations, limiting to an ever-increasing degree the political power of Mohammedanism in Africa, saps the very life of Islam. Christianity must, and will, supplant Mohammedanism in Africa—as a condition of the civilisation of the continent.

We speak as if the civilisation of Africa were

[1] *The Church at Home and Abroad*, viii., 504.

something in the future ; we must not forget
what a start has already been accomplished by
Christianity and commerce—promising completion in a future nearer than perhaps we
imagine. Practically the continent has been
opened but a little more than a quarter of a
century, if it can be called " opened " even now.
Yet it is already almost entirely explored, and
even partitioned. Half the work of civilisation
has been accomplished, in a knowledge of the
interior and in an assurance of Christian control.
In Africa we are not dealing with a conservat-
ive and well-nigh impregnable power, like that
which closes China to Christian civilisation.
Africa, far behind even China a quarter of a
century ago, has in these past few years made a
great leap forward towards Christian civilisation. The slave-trade is already doomed. A
wide-spread and complex commerce has begun
and must enlarge. " The opening of Central
Africa to commerce is working great changes
among the people. They are rapidly laying
aside their native clothing, arms, and imple-
ments, and adopting those brought in from
civilised lands. People that a few years ago

asked the traders for beads, trinkets, and brass
rods, now ask for guns and cloth and—rum."[1]
Together with commerce and political control,
Christianity has already laid its beneficent grasp
upon the continent. Hints of the future solution are given in the magnificent manhood
that has already been shown by some of the
native converts. Once in the heart of Dark
Africa a native was dragged before Mr. Stanley
by some of his followers, for stealing a gun.
Stanley looked at the gun, saw clearly that
it belonged to his expedition. The poor fellow that had it was so frightened that he
could hardly find voice, but stammered, "*I
am a son of God; I would not steal.*"[2] He
had found the gun and was attempting to
return it.

The great solution of the problem, the true
civilisation of Africa, will be accomplished by
commerce and Christianity. Commerce has its
mission, its dangers, its heroism ; but the need
and the greed of man may be trusted to drive
it forward irresistibly. Christianity has already

[1] *The Missionary Review of the World*, i., 374.
[2] *Ibid.*, iv., 638.

called and crowned its heroes; but its mission is also more largely ahead than behind.   It must depend on the heroism of men and women yet to offer themselves, living sacrifices.

INDEX